Ex Libris

LCE

THE
LOREN
EISELEY
READER

Foreword by Ray Bradbury

Illustrations by Aaron Franco

THE LOREN EISELEY SOCIETY &
ABBATIA PRESS
An imprint of Infusionmedia Publishing
Lincoln, Nebraska

First edition

"The Flow of the River," "How Flowers Changed the World," "The Judgment of the Birds" from *The Immense Journey* by Loren Eiseley, originally published by Random House, Inc., copyright 1946, 1950, 1951, 1953, 1955, 1956, 1957 Loren Eiseley.

"The Star Thrower," "The Innocent Fox," "The Last Neanderthal" from *The Unexpected Universe* by Loren Eiseley, originally published by Harcourt Brace & Company, copyright 1964, 1966, 1968, 1969 Loren Eiseley, copyright renewed 1994 John A. Eichman, 3rd.

"Prologue," "The World Eaters," "The Last Magician," "The Spore Bearers" from *The Invisible Pyramid* by Loren Eiseley, originally published by Charles Scribner's Sons, an imprint of Simon & Schuster Inc., copyright 1970 Loren Eiseley.

"The Gold Wheel" from *The Night Country* by Loren Eiseley, originally published by Charles Scribner's Sons, an imprint of Simon & Schuster Inc., copyright 1947, 1948, 1951, 1958, 1962, 1963, 1964, 1966, 1971 Loren Eiseley.

"The Innocent Assassins" from *The Innocent Assassins* by Loren Eiseley, originally published by Charles Scribner's Sons, an imprint of Simon & Schuster Inc., copyright 1973 Loren Eiseley.

All above material reprinted with permission of the Trustee of the Loren Eiseley Estate, University of Pennsylvania Archives and Records Center

ISBN: 978-0-9796586-8-6
Library of Congress Control Number: 2009903961

Cover art and illustrations by Aaron Franco
Typesetting and design by Aaron Vacin
Copyediting by Cris Trautner with assistance
by Aaron Vacin and Deborah Derrick

All photographs are provided courtesy of the University of Pennsylvania Archives unless otherwise noted.

The interior pages of this book are printed on Finch Opaque, a 30 percent recycled post-consumer waste, chlorine-free paper.

The Loren Eiseley Society
www.eiseley.org

Infusionmedia Publishing Inc.
www.infusionmediapublishing.com

Contents

Foreword

Over a period of years, I gave advice to Loren Eiseley, which he indeed took. I read "The Fire Apes" in *Harper's Magazine* many years ago and then sat down and wrote a letter of great affection and appreciation to Loren Eiseley, saying that I thought it was the most extraordinary essay I'd read in many years and that I thought he should write a book. I then sent my letter on to *Harper's Magazine,* hoping that they would pass it on to him.

After a period of months, Loren responded to me, thank God, and said that my suggestion to him to write a book sounded mighty good.

Well, he sat down and within a few years wrote his first book. When it finally came out, I was delighted.

At one point he came to Los Angeles and we had dinner together, and a great friendship resulted from this.

I remember one night I went to hear him lecture at Occidental College. During dinner, he read his speech to the people there and they began to drowse and go to sleep.

When his speech was done, I jumped up on the stage and grabbed his speech and said, "Mr. Eiseley, my God, you must not read your speeches. You must memorize these words and speak directly to the audience, because this is a brilliant speech, just like your essays. You must always keep your eyes on the audience and speak these wonderful words directly to them."

From that point on, Loren was careful to follow my advice and speak his speeches directly to the audience and give his words spontaneously to them.

Over the years, he told me one of the reasons that he and his wife had no children. Apparently, somewhere in his background, there was some sort of mental problem, going back to his parents and grandparents, so he and his wife decided never to have children.

My final message to Loren Eiseley is this:

My dear Loren, you have been gone quite a few years now, but I want to tell you this: You have children. Thank God for that. The essays you've written and the books that you've created are children, so your heritage will go on to the end of this century and to the centuries beyond. You have children, Loren Eiseley, and you will live forever.

Ray Bradbury

Introduction

Loren Eiseley once wrote, "We have joined the caravan, you might say, at a certain point; we will travel as far as we can see, but we cannot in one lifetime see all that we would like to see or learn all that we hunger to know."

This collection of essays is intended to introduce the writings of Nebraska naturalist and philosopher Loren Eiseley to a new generation of readers, and to reach out to old friends who know Eiseley and may wish to sample his essays to gain new perspectives on his work. We hope it will enable readers to join with Eiseley, for a short while, on that caravan ride through an individual life, as well as to gain a sense of what it means to participate in that much longer—indeed that immense— journey of our collective lives that we call evolution.

For our younger readers, we wish to introduce you to a new world of wonder and exploration through Eiseley's eyes. Eiseley grew up in the pre-Depression years of the 1920s in and near Lincoln, Nebraska. In his youth, he wandered through marshes and sewers, explored sunflower forests, filled fish tanks with muck and mire from a frozen pond to see what might emerge, and played dice in an abandoned house near his home. He became fascinated by the mammoth bones he saw on a visit to the state museum, and soon set up a museum of his own discoveries. As a university student, he hunted fossils in the rich bone beds of western Nebraska and eastern Wyoming. These experiences would inspire the essays and poems that he wrote about the mysteries of nature and humankind's relationship to the natural world.

In the classroom, given Eiseley's lyrical writing style and his keen scientific eye, we hope to build a bridge between the sciences and the humanities. Eiseley is best known for his unique concealed-essay style, in which he uses personal anecdotes, reminiscences, allusions, and metaphor to discuss complex scientific ideas and draw ties between the humanities and the sciences. We believe that Eiseley's essays can be used by teachers in many disciplines, including life sciences, anthropology, paleontology, ecology, geology, and English. Educational materials and lesson guides for K-12 grade levels are being developed for teachers to incorporate into their classrooms for each essay in the *Reader*. These materials are available for download from The Loren Eiseley Society Web site (http://www.eiseley.org). Students are also encouraged to visit the Web site's "Young Readers Activities" section.

Noted science fiction author Ray Bradbury has generously written a passionate foreword to this collection of essays. As Eiseley biographer Gale Christianson notes, "Bradbury recognized a fellow storyteller when he saw one." After he read several of Eiseley's essays published in *Harper's Magazine*, Bradbury contacted Eiseley and encouraged him to collect his essays into a single work, which became *The Immense Journey*. *The Immense Journey* is regarded today by *The New York Times* as one of the most influential works of literature of the twentieth century.

The *Reader* is a sampling of Loren Eiseley's works. It is by no means a comprehensive collection of his writing. This volume includes fifteen essays and one poem, which have been carefully selected from Eiseley's numerous books of poetry and prose. The *Reader* is divided into three main sections, giving the teacher or reader an option to focus on an aspect of Eiseley's writing that is deemed most appropriate for the moment at hand. A brief synopsis of the literary pieces in this volume, and the books from which they are taken, is given here.

> "Prologue"—the need for humankind to rediscover and reenter the natural world, symbolized by the sunflower forest (*The Invisible Pyramid*).

"The Slit"—a discovery reveals a power from which humanity may acquire wisdom (*The Immense Journey*).

"The Flow of the River"—the power of flowing water in the shaping of continents in an endless cycle of creation and destruction (*The Immense Journey*).

"How Flowers Changed the World"—the rise of the first flowers during the Cretaceous period was a precursor to the end of the dinosaurs and the eventual rise of the mammals (*The Immense Journey*).

"The Judgment of the Birds"—speaks to the commitment to life by a flock of birds in spite of a tragedy to one of their own kind (*The Immense Journey*).

"The Innocent Assassins"—a poem written after the discovery of the fossil of two saber-toothed cats locked in a life-death struggle by Eiseley's archaeological team in the Wildcat Hills of western Nebraska (*The Innocent Assassins*).

"The Gold Wheel"—recounts Eiseley's childhood discovery of a golden wheel and his search for its twin; a metaphor for humankind's search for the holy grail (*The Night Country*).

"The Running Man"—describes events and reminiscences from Eiseley's childhood that stirred his wanderlust and desire for escape (*All the Strange Hours*).

"The Letter"—a letter from an old friend moves Eiseley to reflect on the importance of following his own path in life rather than meeting others' expectations (*All the Strange Hours*).

"The Star Thrower"—recounts Eiseley observing an elderly person walking along a beach and deliberately tossing starfish back into the sea as a metaphor for humanity to be the good steward to all life (*The Unexpected Universe*).

"The Last Neanderthal"—as a fossil hunter at a rhino dig near the Wildcat Hills, Eiseley encounters what he imagines to be a haunting throwback to an earlier time during the ice age (*The Unexpected Universe*).

"The Innocent Fox"—a chance encounter of play between Eiseley and a cub fox (*The Unexpected Universe*).

"The World Eaters"—can humankind's rapaciousness and insatiable consumption of the earth's resources be sustained? (*The Invisible Pyramid*).

"The Spore Bearers"—analogous to soaring rockets into space is the cap thrower fungus, which in its last act of life shoots its spores into space (*The Invisible Pyramid*).

"The Last Magician"—a survival guide to humanity's tenure on Earth (*The Invisible Pyramid*).

Loren Eiseley has been described as "a man who can see through time" and as a "modern shaman." In light of our current and impending global environmental crises, Eiseley's words are more relevant than ever as we grapple with the many issues facing humanity in the twenty-first century. Our precious planet is an insignificant pale blue dot in the vastness of space, rotating around an average star located in the outskirts of an average galaxy, which is a member of a local group of galaxies. Yet within this vastness of space, born of third-generation star stuff, Man the lonely has arisen to join the Caravan. To stay with the caravan, Eiseley provides us with his wise counsel: "We know that within our heads there still exists an irrational restive ghost that can whisper disastrous messages into the ear of reason. Today man's mounting numbers and his technological power to pollute his environment reveal a single demanding necessity: the necessity for him consciously to reenter ... into the sunflower forest... Man must be his last magician. He must seek his own way home."

Bing Chen
The Loren Eiseley Society

Biography

Loren Corey Eiseley likened the brain of a writer to "an unseen artist's loft," in which "pictures from the past" were stored and brought forth to be magnified or reduced in order to form a pattern. Many of the patterns he created in his work were associated with his experiences during his years growing up in his prairie state, Nebraska. The land, the people, and the institutions left an ineradicable mark upon him and colored what he did.

Born in 1907 in Lincoln, he spent his first crucial years in the eastern part of the state, only leaving in 1933 to begin graduate study in anthropology. His time was characterized by the end of pioneer days in the Midwest, the growth of towns and cities, and the accumulation of wealth. The capital city, in which he spent most of those early years, doubled in population. In the twenty-six years from 1907 to 1933, Lincoln grew from 40,000 to 80,000 residents, and it was in those years that the schools, museums, and libraries that were so important to him were established.

The Eiseley family had always lived on the edge of town, somewhat removed from the people and the community from which they felt set apart through poverty and family misfortune. This setting, however, opened the adjacent country to a wandering boy with an early interest in the natural world. It was to this world he turned for the satisfactions he did not find at home. It provided easy access to the pond where he collected specimens for his aquarium, to the cave in the creek bank, and to other locations that would eventually find their way into his writings. He described the lands around Lincoln as "flat and grass covered and smiling so serenely up at the sun that they seemed forever writings. He described the lands around Lincoln as "flat and grass covered and smiling so serenely up at the sun that they seemed forever youthful, untouched by mind or time—a sunlit, timeless prairie over which nothing passed but antelope or wandering bird."

Loren Eiseley's father, Clyde, worked as a hardware salesman with long hours and little remuneration. A sometimes amateur Shakespearian actor, he gave his son a love for beautiful language and writing. The tie between father and son was close—he thought that Loren was a "genius, but moody."

His mother, Daisey Corey, was described as "an untaught prairie artist." She was a beautiful woman who had lost her hearing in childhood and was locked in a silent world. Given at times to irrational, destructive behavior, she communicated with her son by thumping on the floor. It was an unhappy marriage that left its mark on the young child, who felt forever alienated from his mother.

But, in spite of this, there were other people in his world who opened the door to a happier life. His half brother, Leo, gave him a copy of *Robinson Crusoe* with which he taught himself to read. His Uncle Buck and Aunt Grace, who lived nearby, opened their home to him and helped him financially. The former took him to the natural history museum, Morrill Hall, where the fossils fascinated him and led him to his future career. He made Neanderthal heads from clay and, with the help of his grandmother, Melinda Corey, baked them in the kitchen oven and stored them in a nearby barn. Somehow he found his way to the public library and became a voracious reader.

Eiseley attended the Lincoln Public Schools, where in high school he wrote that he wanted to be a nature writer. Disturbed by his home situation and the illness and death of his father, he dropped out of school and worked at menial jobs while trying to avoid the truant officer. He enrolled in the University of Nebraska, wrote for the newly formed *Prairie Schooner*, and went on digs for the museum. His education was interrupted by tuberculosis for which an enforced stay in the mountains and desert was mandated. In addition, his restlessness and unhappiness resulted in a year of riding the rails all over the West. Finally, in 1933, he was awarded a B.S. degree in English and geology/anthropology.

Eiseley went on to secure his master's and Ph.D. in anthropology from the University of Pennsylvania and to do post-doctoral work at Columbia University. He taught at the University of Kansas and at Oberlin College, and then returned in 1949 to the faculty at the University of Pennsylvania, where he worked until his death.

In 1938, Eiseley married Mabel Langden of Nebraska. It was a childless marriage in which she devoted her entire life to her husband and his career, a career marked by increasing fame as a writer, science educator, teacher, and philosopher. In 1942, the *Scientific American* published his first popular essay, "The Folsum Mystery," which was the forerunner of the later personal essays for which he is best known. These essays deal with the history of civilization and our relationship with the natural world.

It was the publication in 1946 of his first and best-known book, *The Immense Journey*, that established him as a writer with the unique ability to combine science and humanism. *The Immense Journey* is a collection of essays, many of which owe their origin to his early Nebraska experiences. From that point on, he was recognized nationally and internationally and given major prizes and honorary degrees.

When Loren Eiseley was three, his father held him up to watch Halley's Comet blaze across the sky and told him to look for its return in seventy-five years. But Loren Eiseley did not live that long. He died July 9, 1977, having used his brief seventy years to leave behind a heritage that continues to enrich the lives of all who come to know his work.

Naomi Brill
The Loren Eiseley Society

Prologue from *The Invisible Pyramid*

Once in a cycle the comet
Doubles its lonesome track.
Enriched with tears of
a thousand years,
Aeschylus wanders back.

JOHN G. NEIHARDT

Man would not be man if his dreams did not exceed his grasp. If, in this book, I choose to act in the ambivalent character of pessimist and optimist, it is because mankind itself plays a similar contradictory role upon the stage of life. Like John Donne, man lies in a close prison, yet it is dear to him. Like Donne's, his thoughts at times overleap the sun and pace beyond the body. If I term humanity a slime mold organism it is because our present environment suggests it. If I remember the sunflower forest it is because from its hidden reaches man arose. The green world is his sacred center. In moments of sanity he must still seek refuge there.

If I dream by contrast of the eventual drift of the star voyagers through the dilated time of the universe, it is because I have seen thistledown off to new worlds and am at heart a voyager who, in this modern time, still yearns for the lost country of his birth. As an anthropologist I know that we exist in the morning twilight of humanity and pray that we may survive its noon. The travail of the men of my profession is to delve amid the fragments of civilizations irretrievably lost and, at the same time, to know man's enormous capacity to create.

But I dream, and because I dream, I severally condemn, fear, and salute the future. It is the salute of a gladiator ringed by the indifference of the watching stars. Man himself is the solitary arbiter of his own defeats and victories. I have mused on the dead of all epochs from flint to steel. They fought blindly and well against the future, or the cities and ourselves would not be here. Now all about us, unseen, the final desperate engagement continues.

If man goes down I do not believe that he will ever again have the resources or the strength to defend the sunflower forest and simultaneously to follow the beckoning road across the star fields. It is now or never for both, and the price is very high. It may be, as A. E. Housman said, that we breathe the air that kills both at home and afar. He did not speak of pollution; he spoke instead of the death that comes with memory. I have wondered how long the social memory of a great culture can be sustained without similarly growing lethal. This also our century may decide.

I confess that the air that kills has been breathed upon the pages of this book, but upon it also has shone the silver light of flying thistledown. In the heart of the city I have heard the wild geese crying on the pathways that lie over a vanished forest. Nature has not changed the force that drives them. Man, too, is a different expression of that natural force. He has fought his way from the sea's depths to Palomar Mountain. He has mastered the plague. Now, in some final Armageddon, he confronts himself.

As a boy I once rolled dice in an empty house, playing against myself. I suppose I was afraid. It was twilight, and I forget who won. I was too young to have known that the old abandoned house in which I played was the universe. I would play for man more fiercely if the years would take me back.

Reflections of a Naturalist

The Slit

Man can not afford to be a naturalist, to look at
Nature directly, but only with the side of his eye.
He must look through and beyond her.

HENRY DAVID THOREAU

Unless all existence is a medium of revelation,
no particular revelation is possible...

WILLIAM TEMPLE

Some lands are flat and grass-covered, and smile so evenly up at the
sun that they seem forever youthful, untouched by man or time. Some
are torn, ravaged and convulsed like the features of profane old age.
Rocks are wrenched up and exposed to view; black pits receive the sun
but give back no light.

It was to such a land I rode, but I rode to it across a sunlit, timeless
prairie over which nothing passed but antelope or a wandering bird.
On the verge where that prairie halted before a great wall of naked
sandstone and clay, I came upon the Slit. A narrow crack worn by some
descending torrent had begun secretly, far back in the prairie grass,
and worked itself deeper and deeper into the fine sandstone that led
by devious channels into the broken waste beyond. I rode back along

the crack to a spot where I could descend into it, dismounted and left my horse to graze.

The crack was only about body-width and, as I worked my way downward, the light turned dark and green from the overhanging grass. Above me the sky became a narrow slit of distant blue, and the sandstone was cool to my hands on either side. The Slit was a little sinister—like an open grave, assuming the dead were enabled to take one last look—for over me the sky seemed already as far off as some future century I would never see.

I ignored the sky, then, and began to concentrate on the sandstone walls that had led me into this place. It was tight and tricky work, but that cut was a perfect cross section through perhaps ten million years of time. I hoped to find at least a bone, but I was not quite prepared for the sight I finally came upon. Staring straight out at me, as I slid farther and deeper into the green twilight, was a skull embedded in the solid sandstone. I had come at just the proper moment when it was fully to be seen, the white bone gleaming there in a kind of ashen splendor, water worn, and about to be ground away in the next long torrent.

It was not, of course, human. I was deep, deep below the time of man in a remote age near the beginning of the reign of mammals . I squatted on my heels in the narrow ravine, and we stared a little blankly at each other, the skull and I. There were marks of generalized primitives in that low, pinched brain case and grinning jaw that marked it as laying far back along those converging roads where, as I shall have occasion to establish elsewhere, cat and man and weasel must leap into a single shape.

It was the face of a creature who had spent his days following his nose, who was led by instinct rather than memory, and whose power of choice was very small. Though he was not a man, nor a direct human ancestor, there was yet about him, even in the bone, some trace of that low, snuffling world out of which our forebears had so recently emerged. The skull lay tilted in such a manner that it stared, sightless, up at me as though I, too, were already caught a few feet above him in the strata and, in my turn, were staring upward at the strip of sky which the ages were carrying farther away from me beneath the tumbling debris of falling mountains. The creature had never lived to see a man, and I, what was it I was never going to see?

I restrained a panicky impulse to hurry upward after the receding sky that was outlined above the Slit. Probably, I thought, as I patiently began the task of chiseling into the stone around the skull, I would never again excavate a fossil under conditions which led to so vivid an impression that I was already one myself. The truth is that we are all potential fossils still carrying within our bodies the crudities of former existences, the marks of a world in which living creatures flow with little more consistency than clouds from age to age.

As I tapped and chiseled there in the foundations of the world, I had ample time to consider the cunning manipulability of the human fingers. Experimentally I crooked one of the long slender bones. It might have been silica, I thought, or aluminum, or iron—the cells would have made it possible. But no, it is calcium, carbonate of lime. Why? Only because of its history. Elements more numerous than calcium in the earth's crust could have been used to build the skeleton. Our history is the reason—we came from the water. It was there the cells took the lime habit, and they kept it after we came ashore.

It is not a bad symbol of that long wandering, I thought again—the human hand that has been fin and scaly reptile foot and furry paw. If a stone should fall (I cocked an eye at the leaning shelf above my head and waited, fatalistically) let the bones lie here with their message, for those who might decipher it, if they come down late among us from the stars.

Above me the great crack seemed to lengthen.

Perhaps there is no meaning in it at all, the thought went on inside me, save that of journey itself, so far as men can see. It has altered with the chances of life, and the chances brought us here; but it was a good journey—long, perhaps—but a good journey under a pleasant sun. Do not look for the purpose. Think of the way we came and be a little proud. Think of this hand—the utter pain of its first venture on the pebbly shore.

Or consider its later wanderings.

I ceased my tappings around the sand-filled sockets of the skull and wedged myself into a crevice for a smoke. As I tamped a load of tobacco into my pipe, I thought of a town across the valley that I used sometimes to visit, a town whose little inhabitants never welcomed me. No sign points to it and I rarely go there any more. Few people know about it and fewer still know that in a sense we, or rather some of the creatures to whom we are related, were driven out of it once, long ago. I used to park my car on a hill and sit silently observant, listening to the talk ringing out from neighbor to neighbor, seeing the inhabitants drowsing in their doorways, taking it all in with nostalgia—the sage smell on the wind, the sunlight without time, the village without destiny. We can look, but we can never go back. It is prairie-dog town.

"Whirl is king," said Aristophanes, and never since life began was Whirl more truly king than eighty million years ago in the dawn of the Age of Mammals. It would come as a shock to those who believe firmly that the scroll of the future is fixed and the roads determined in advance, to observe the teetering balance of earth's history through the age of the Paleocene. The passing of the reptiles had left a hundred uninhabited life zones and a scrambling variety of newly radiating forms. Unheard-of species of giant ground birds threatened for a moment to dominate the earthly scene. Two separate orders of life contended at slightly different intervals for the pleasant grasslands—for the seeds and the sleepy burrows in the sun.

Sometimes, sitting there in the mountain sunshine above prairie-dog town, I could imagine the attraction of that open world after the fern forest damp or the croaking gloom of carboniferous swamps.

There by a tree root I could almost make him out, that shabby little Paleocene rat, eternal tramp and world wanderer, father of all mankind. He ruffled his coat in the sun and hopped forward for a seed. It was to be a long time before he would be seen on the grass again, but he was trying to make up his mind. For good or ill there was to be one more chance, but that chance was fifty million years away.

Here in the Paleocene occurred the first great radiation of the placental mammals, and among them were the earliest primates—the zoological order to which man himself belongs. Today, with a few unimportant exceptions, the primates are all arboreal in habit except man. For this reason we have tended to visualize all of our remote relatives as tree dwellers. Recent discoveries, however, have begun to alter this one-sided picture. Before the rise of the true rodents, the highly successful order to which present-day prairie dogs and chipmunks belong, the environment which they occupy had remained peculiarly open to exploitation. Into this zone crowded a varied assemblage of our early relatives.

"In habitat," comments one scholar, "many of these early primates may be thought of as the rats of the Paleocene. With the later appearance of true rodents, the primate habitat was markedly restricted." The bone hunters, in other words, have succeeded in demonstrating that numerous primates reveal a remarkable development of rodent-like characteristics in the teeth and skull during this early period of mammalian evolution. The movement is progressive and distributed in several different groups. One form, although that of a true primate, shows similarities to the modern kangaroo rat, which is, of course, a rodent. There is little doubt that it was a burrower.

It is this evidence of a lost chapter in the history of our kind that I used to remember on the sunny slope above prairie-dog town, and that enables me to say in a somewhat figurative fashion that we were driven out of it once ages ago. We are not, except very remotely as mammals, related to prairie dogs. Nevertheless, through several million years of Paleocene time, the primate order, instead of being confined to trees, was experimenting to some extent with the same grassland burrowing life that the rodents later perfected. The success of these burrowers crowded the primates out of this environment and forced them back into the domain of the branches. As a result, many primates, by that time highly specialized for a ground life, became extinct.

In the restricted world of the trees, a "refuge area," as the zoologist would say, the others lingered on in diminished numbers. Our ancient relatives, it appeared, were beaten in their attempt to expand upon the ground; they were dying out in the temperate zone, and their significance as a widespread and diversified group was fading. The shabby pseudo-rat I had seen ruffling his coat to dry after the night damps of the reptile age, had ascended again into the green twilight of the rain forest. The chatterers with the ever-growing teeth were his masters. The sunlight and the grass belonged to them.

It is conceivable that except for the invasion of the rodents, the primate line might even have abandoned the trees. We might be there on the grass, you and I, barking in the high-plains sunlight. It is true we came back in fifty million years with the cunning hands and the eyes that the tree world gave us, but was it victory? Once more in memory I saw the high blue evening fall sleepily upon that village, and once more swung the car to leave, lifting, as I always did, a figurative lantern to some ambiguous crossroads sign within my brain. The pointing arms were nameless and nameless were the distances to which they pointed. One took one's choice.

I ceased my daydreaming then, squeezed myself out of the crevice, shook out my pipe, and started chipping once more, the taps sounding along the inward-leaning walls of the Slit like the echo of many footsteps ascending and descending. I had come a long way down since morning; I had projected myself across a dimension I was not fitted to traverse in the flesh. In the end I collected my tools and climbed painfully up through the colossal debris of ages. When I put my hands on the surface of the crack I looked all about carefully in a sudden anxiety that it might not be a grazing horse that I would see.

He had not visibly changed, however, and I mounted in some slight trepidation and rode off, having a memory for a camp—if I had gotten a foot in the right era—which should lie somewhere over to the west. I did not, however, escape totally from that brief imprisonment.

Perhaps the Slit, with its exposed bones and its far-off vanishing sky, has come to stand symbolically in my mind for a dimension denied to man, the dimension of time. Like the wistaria on the garden wall he is rooted in his particular century. Out of it—forward or backward— he cannot run. As he stands on his circumscribed pinpoint of time, his sight for the past is growing longer, and even the shadowy outlines of the galactic future are growing clearer, though his own fate he cannot yet see. Along the dimension of time, man, like the rooted vine in space, may never pass in person. Considering the innumerable devices by which the mindless root has evaded the limitations of its own stability, however, it may well be that man himself is slowly achieving powers over a new dimension—a dimension capable of presenting him with a wisdom he has barely begun to discern.

Through how many dimensions and how many media will life have to pass? Down how many roads among the stars must man propel himself in search of the final secret? The journey is difficult, immense, at times impossible, yet that will not deter some of us from attempting it. We cannot know all that has happened in the past, or the reason for all of these events, any more that we can with surety discern what lies ahead. We have joined the caravan, you might say, at a certain point; we will travel as far as we can, but we cannot in one lifetime see all that we would like to see or learn all that we hunger to know.

The reader who would pursue such a journey with me is warned that essays in this book [*The Immense Journey*] have not been brought together as a guide but are offered rather as a somewhat unconventional record of the prowlings of one mind which has sought to explore, to understand, and to enjoy the miracles of this world, both in and out of science. It is, without doubt, an inconsistent record in many ways, compounded of fear and hope, for it has grown out of the seasonal jottings of a man preoccupied with time. It involves, I see now as I come to put it together, the four ancient elements of the Greeks: mud and the fire within it we call life, vast waters, and something— space, air, the intangible substance of hope which at the last proves unanalyzable by science, yet out of which the human dream is made.

Forward and backward I have gone, and for me it has been an immense journey. Those who accompany me need not look for science in the usual sense, though I have done all in my power to avoid errors in fact. I have given the record of what one man thought as he pursued research and pressed his hands against the confining walls of scientific method in his time. It is not, I must confess at the outset, an account of discovery so much as a confession of ignorance and of the final illumination that sometimes comes to a man when he is no longer careful of his pride. In the last three chapters of the book I have tried to put down such miracles as can be evoked from common earth. But men see differently. I can at best report only from my own wilderness. The important thing is that each man possess such a wilderness and that he consider what marvels are to be observed there.

Finally, I do not pretend to have set down, in Baconian terms, a true, or even a consistent model of the universe. I can only say that here is a bit of my personal universe, the universe traversed in a long and uncompleted journey. If my record, like those of the sixteenth-century voyagers, is confused by strange beasts or monstrous thoughts or sights of abortive men, these are no more than my eyes saw or my mind conceived. On the world island we are all castaways, so that what is seen by one may often be dark or obscure to another.

The Flow of the River

If there is magic on this planet, it is contained in water. Its least stir even, as now in a rain pond on a flat roof opposite my office, is enough to bring me searching to the window. A wind ripple may be translating itself into life. I have a constant feeling that some time I may witness that momentous miracle on a city roof, see life veritably and suddenly boiling out of a heap of rusted pipes and old television aerials. I marvel at how suddenly a water beetle has come and is submarining there in a spatter of green algae. Thin vapors, rust, wet tar and sun are an alembic remarkably like the mind; they throw off odorous shadows that threaten to take real shape when no one is looking.

Once in a lifetime, perhaps, one escapes the actual confines of the flesh. Once in a lifetime, if one is lucky, one so merges with sunlight and air and running water that whole eons, the eons that mountains and deserts know, might pass in a single afternoon without discomfort. The mind has sunk away into its beginnings among old roots and the obscure tricklings and movings that stir inanimate things. Like the charmed fairy circle into which a man once stepped, and upon emergence learned that a whole century had passed in a single night, one can never quite define this secret; but it has something to do, I am sure, with common water. Its substance reaches everywhere; it touches the past and prepares the future; it moves under the poles and wanders thinly in the heights of air. It can assume forms of exquisite perfection in a snowflake, or strip the living to a single shining bone cast up by the sea.

Many years ago, in the course of some scientific investigations in a remote western county, I experienced, by chance, precisely the sort of curious absorption by water—the extension of shape by osmosis—at which I have been hinting. You have probably never experienced in yourself the meandering roots of a whole watershed or felt your out-stretched fingers touching, by some kind of clairvoyant extension, the brooks of snow-line glaciers at the same time that you were flowing toward the Gulf over the eroded debris of worn-down mountains. A poet, MacKnight Black, has spoken of being "limbed ... with waters gripping pole and pole." He had the idea, all right, and it is obvious that these sensations are not unique, but they are hard to come by; and the sort of extension of the senses that people will accept when they put their ear against a sea shell, they will smile at in the confessions of a bookish professor. What makes it worse is the fact that because of a traumatic experience in childhood, I am not a swimmer, and am in-clined to be timid before any large body of water. Perhaps it was just this, in a way, that contributed to my experience.

As it leaves the Rockies and moves downward over the high plains towards the Missouri, the Platte River is a curious stream. In the spring floods, on occasion, it can be a mile-wide roaring torrent of destruc-tion, gulping farms and bridges. Normally, however, it is a rambling, dispersed series of streamlets flowing erratically over great sand and gravel fans that are, in part, the remnants of a mightier Ice Age stream bed. Quicksands and shifting islands haunt its waters. Over it the prairie suns beat mercilessly throughout the summer. The Platte, "a mile wide and an inch deep," is a refuge for any heat-weary pilgrim along its shores. This is particularly true on the high plains before its long march by the cities begins.

The reason that I came upon it when I did, breaking through a wil-low thicket and stumbling out through ankle-deep water to a dune in the shade, is of no concern to this narrative. On various purposes of science I have ranged over a good bit of that country on foot, and I know the kinds of bones that come gurgling up through the gravel pumps, and the arrowheads of shining chalcedony that occasionally spill out of water-loosened sand. On that day, however, the sight of sky and willows and the weaving net of water murmuring a little in the shallows on its way to the Gulf stirred me, parched as I was with miles of walking, with a new idea: I was going to float. I was going to undergo a tremendous adventure.

The notion came to me, I suppose, by degrees. I had shed my clothes and was floundering pleasantly in a hole among some reeds when a great desire to stretch out and go with this gently insistent water began to pluck at me. Now to this bronzed, bold, modern generation, the struggle I waged with timidity while standing there in knee-deep water can only seem farcical; yet actually for me it was not so. A near-drowning accident in childhood had scarred my reactions; in addition to the fact that I was a nonswimmer, this "inch-deep river" was treacherous with holes and quicksands. Death was not precisely infrequent along its wandering and illusory channels. Like all broad wastes of this kind, where neither water nor land quite prevails, its thickets were lonely and untraversed. A man in trouble would cry out in vain.

I thought of all this, standing quietly in the water, feeling the sand shifting away under my toes. Then I lay back in the floating position that left my face to the sky, and shoved off. The sky wheeled over me. For an instant, as I bobbed into the main channel, I had the sensation of sliding down the vast tilted face of the continent. It was then that I felt the cold needles of the alpine springs at my fingertips, and the warmth of the Gulf pulling me southward. Moving with me, leaving its taste upon my mouth and spouting under me in dancing springs of sand, was the immense body of the continent itself, flowing like the river was flowing, grain by grain, mountain by mountain, down to the sea. I was streaming over ancient sea beds thrust aloft where giant reptiles had once sported; I was wearing down the face of time and trundling cloud-wreathed ranges into oblivion. I touched my margins with the delicacy of a crayfish's antennae, and felt great fishes glide about their work.

I drifted by stranded timber cut by beaver in mountain fastnesses; I slid over shallows that had buried the broken axles of prairie schooners and the mired bones of mammoth. I was streaming alive through the hot and working ferment of the sun, or oozing secretively through shady thickets. I *was* water and the unspeakable alchemies that gestate and take shape in water, the slimy jellies that under the enormous magnification of the sun writhe and whip upward as great barbeled fish mouths, or sink indistinctly back into the murk out of which they arose. Turtle and fish and the pinpoint chirpings of individual frogs are all watery projections, concentrations—as man himself is a concentration—of that indescribable and liquid brew which is compounded in varying proportions of salt and sun and time. It has appearances, but at its heart lies water, and as I was finally edged gently against a sand bar and dropped like any log, I tottered as I rose. I knew once more the body's revolt against emergence into the harsh and unsupporting air, its reluctance to break contact with that mother element which still, at this late point in time, shelters and brings into being nine tenths of everything alive.

As for men, those myriad little detached ponds with their own swarming corpuscular life, what were they but a way that water has of going about beyond the reach of rivers? I, too, was a microcosm of pouring rivulets and floating driftwood gnawed by the mysterious animalcules of my own creation. I was three fourths water, rising and subsiding according to the hollow knocking in my veins: a minute pulse like the eternal pulse that lifts Himalayas and which, in the following systole, will carry them away.

Thoreau, peering at the emerald pickerel in Walden Pond, called them "animalized water" in one of his moments of strange insight. If he had been possessed of the geological knowledge so laboriously accumulated since his time, he might have gone further and amusedly detected in the planetary rumblings and eructations which so delighted him in the gross habits of certain frogs, signs of that dark interior stress which has reared sea bottoms up to mountainous heights. He might have developed an acute inner ear for the sound of the surf on Cretaceous beaches where now the wheat of Kansas rolls. In any case, he would have seen, as the long trail of life was unfolded by the fossil hunters, that his animalized water had changed its shapes eon by eon to the beating of the earth's dark millennial heart. In the swamps of the low continents, the amphibians had flourished and had their day; and as the long skyward swing—the isostatic response of the crust—had come about, the era of the cooling grasslands and mammalian life had come into being.

A few winters ago, clothed heavily against the weather, I wandered several miles along one of the tributaries of that same Platte I had floated down years before. The land was stark and ice-locked. The rivulets were frozen, and over the marshlands the willow thickets made such an array of vertical lines against the snow that tramping through them produced strange optical illusions and dizziness. On the edge of a frozen backwater, I stopped and rubbed my eyes. At my feet a raw prairie wind had swept the ice clean of snow. A peculiar green object caught my eye; there was no mistaking it.

Staring up at me with all his barbels spread pathetically, frozen solidly in the wind-ruffled ice, was a huge familiar face. It was one of those catfish of the twisting channels, those dwellers in the yellow murk, who had been about me and beneath me on the day of my great voyage. Whatever sunny dream had kept him paddling there while the mercury plummeted downward and that Cheshire smile froze slowly, it would be hard to say. Or perhaps he was trapped in a blocked channel and had simply kept swimming until the ice contracted around him. At any rate, there he would lie till the spring thaw.

At that moment I started to turn away, but something in the bleak, whiskered face reproached me, or perhaps it was the river calling to her children. I termed it science, however—a convenient rational phrase I reserve for such occasions—and decided that I would cut the fish out of the ice and take him home. I had no intention of eating him. I was merely struck by a sudden impulse to test the survival qualities of high-plains fishes, particularly fishes of this type who get themselves immured in oxygenless ponds or in cut-off oxbows buried in winter drifts. I blocked him out as gently as possible and dropped him, ice and all, into a collecting can in the car. Then we set out for home.

Unfortunately, the first stages of what was to prove a remarkable resurrection escaped me. Cold and tired after a long drive, I deposited the can with its melting water and ice in the basement. The accompanying corpse I anticipated I would either dispose of or dissect on the following day. A hurried glance had revealed no signs of life.

To my astonishment, however, upon descending into the basement several hours later, I heard stirrings in the receptacle and peered in. The ice had melted. A vast pouting mouth ringed with sensitive feelers confronted me, and the creature's gills labored slowly. A thin stream of silver bubbles rose to the surface and popped. A fishy eye gazed up at me protestingly.

"A tank," it said. This was no Walden pickerel. This was a yellow-green, mud-grubbing, evil-tempered inhabitant of floods and droughts and cyclones. It was the selective product of the high continent and the waters that pour across it. It had outlasted prairie blizzards that left cattle standing frozen upright in the drifts.

"I'll get the tank," I said respectfully.

He lived with me all that winter, and his departure was totally in keeping with his sturdy, independent character. In the spring a migratory impulse or perhaps sheer boredom struck him. Maybe, in some little lost corner of his brain, he felt, far off, the pouring of the mountain waters through the sandy coverts of the Platte. Anyhow, something called to him, and he went. One night when no one was about, he simply jumped out of his tank. I found him dead on the floor next morning. He had made his gamble like a man—or, I should say, a fish. In the proper place it would not have been a fool's gamble. Fishes in the drying shallows of intermittent prairie streams who feel their confinement and have the impulse to leap while there is yet time may regain the main channel and survive. A million ancestral years had gone into that jump, I thought as I looked at him, a million years of climbing through prairie sunflowers and twining in and out through the pillared legs of drinking mammoth.

"Some of your close relatives have been experimenting with air breathing," I remarked, apropos of nothing, as I gathered him up. "Suppose we meet again up there in the cottonwoods in a million years or so."

I missed him a little as I said it. He had for me the kind of lost archaic glory that comes from the water brotherhood. We were both projections out of that timeless ferment and locked as well in some greater unity that lay incalculably beyond us. In many a fin and reptile foot I have seen myself passing by—some part of myself, that is, some part that lies unrealized in the momentary shape I inhabit. People have occasionally written me harsh letters and castigated me for a lack of faith in man when I have ventured to speak of this matter in print. They distrust, it would seem, all shapes and thoughts but their own. They would bring God into the compass of a shopkeeper's understanding and confine Him to those limits, lest He proceed to some unimaginable and shocking act—create perhaps, as a casual afterthought, a being more beautiful than man. As for me, I believe nature capable of this, and having been part of the flow of the river, I feel no envy—any more than the frog envies the reptile or an ancestral ape should envy man.

Every spring in the wet meadows and ditches I hear a little shrilling chorus which sounds for all the world like an endlessly reiterated

"We're here, we're here, we're here." And so they are, as frogs, of course. Confident little fellows. I suspect that to some greater ear than ours, man's optimistic pronouncements about his role and destiny may make a similar little ringing sound that travels a small way out into the night. It is only its nearness that is offensive. From the heights of a mountain, or a marsh at evening, it blends, not too badly, with all the other sleepy voices that, in croaks or chirrups, are saying the same thing.

After a while the skilled listener can distinguish man's noise from the katydid's rhythmic assertion, allow for the offbeat of a rabbit's thumping, pick up the autumnal monotone of crickets, and find in all of them a grave pleasure without admitting any to a place of preeminence in his thoughts. It is when all these voices cease and the waters are still, when along the frozen river nothing cries, screams or howls, that the enormous mindlessness of space settles down upon the soul. Somewhere out in that waste of crushed ice and reflected stars, the black waters may be running, but they appear to be running without life toward a destiny in which the whole of space may be locked in some silvery winter of dispersed radiation.

It is then, when the wind comes straitly across the barren marshes and the snow rises and beats in endless waves against the traveler, that I remember best, by some trick of the imagination, my summer voyage on the river. I remember my green extensions, my catfish nuzzlings and minnow wrigglings, my gelatinous materializations out of the mother ooze. And as I walk on through the white smother, it is the magic of water that leaves me a final sign.

Men talk much of matter and energy, of the struggle for existence that molds the shape of life. These things exist, it is true; but more delicate, elusive, quicker than the fins in water, is that mysterious principle known as "organization," which leaves all other mysteries concerned with life stale and insignificant by comparison. For that without organization life does not persist is obvious. Yet this organization itself is not strictly the product of life, nor of selection. Like some dark and passing shadow within matter, it cups out the eyes' small windows or spaces the notes of a meadow lark's song in the interior of a mottled egg. That principle—I am beginning to suspect—was there before the living in the deeps of water.

The temperature has risen. The little stinging needles have given way to huge flakes floating in like white leaves blown from some great tree in open space. In the car, switching on the lights, I examine one intricate crystal on my sleeve before it melts. No utilitarian philosophy explains a snow crystal, no doctrine of use or disuse. Water has merely leapt out of vapor and thin nothingness in the night sky to array itself in form. There is no logical reason for the existence of a snowflake any more than there is for evolution. It is an apparition from that mysterious shadow world beyond nature, that final world which contains—if anything contains—the explanation of men and catfish and green leaves.

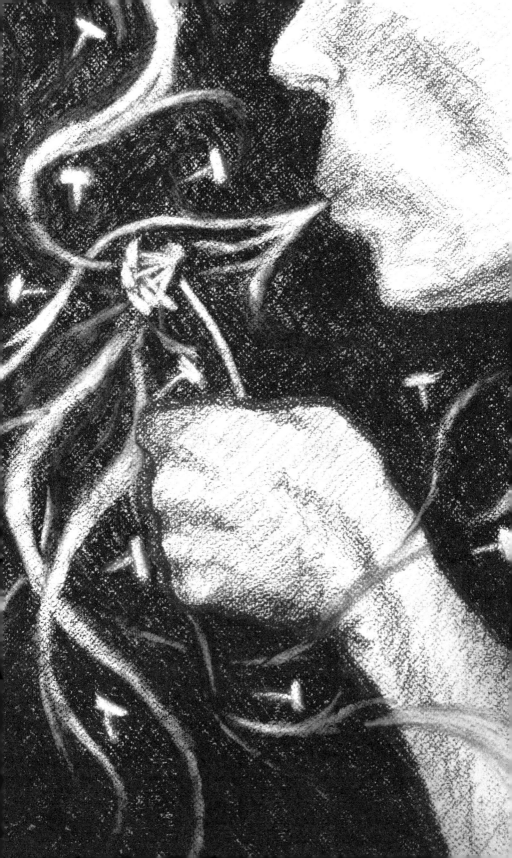

How Flowers Changed the World

If it had been possible to observe the Earth from the far side of the solar system over the long course of geological epochs, the watchers might have been able to discern a subtle change in the light emanating from our planet. That world of long ago would, like the red deserts of Mars, have reflected light from vast drifts of stone and gravel, the sands of wandering wastes, the blackness of naked basalt, the yellow dust of endlessly moving storms. Only the ceaseless marching of the clouds and the intermittent flashes from the restless surface of the sea would have told a different story, but still essentially a barren one. Then, as the millennia rolled away and age followed age, a new and greener light would, by degrees, have come to twinkle across those endless miles.

This is the only difference those far watchers, by the use of the subtle instruments, might have perceived in the whole history of the planet Earth. Yet that slowly growing green twinkle would have contained the epic march of life from the tidal oozes upward across the raw and unclothed continents. Out of the vast chemical bath of the sea—not from the deeps, but from the element-rich, light-exposed platforms of the continental shelves—wandering fingers of green had crept upward along the meanderings of river systems and fringed the gravels of forgotten lakes.

In those first ages plants clung of necessity to swamps and watercourses. Their reproductive processes demanded direct access to water. Beyond the primitive ferns and mosses that enclosed the borders of swamps and streams the rocks still lay vast and bare, the winds still swirled the dust of a naked planet. The grass cover that holds our world secure in place was still millions of years in the future. The green marchers had gained a soggy foothold upon the land, but that was all. They did not reproduce by seeds but by microscopic swimming sperm that had to wriggle their way through water to fertilize the female cell. Such plants in their higher forms had clever adaptations for the use of rain water in their sexual phases, and survived with increasing success in wet land environment. They now seem part of man's normal environment. The truth is, however, that there is nothing very "normal" about nature. Once upon a time there were no flowers at all.

A little while ago—about one hundred million years, as the geologist estimates time in the history of our four-billion-year-old planet— flowers were not to be found anywhere on the five continents. Wherever one might have looked, from the poles to the equator, one would have seen only the cold dark monotonous green of a world whose plant life possessed no other color.

Somewhere, just a short time before the close of the Age of Reptiles, there occurred a soundless, violent explosion. It lasted millions of years, but it was an explosion, nevertheless. It marked the emergence of the angiosperms—the flowering plants. Even the great evolutionist Charles Darwin called them "an abominable mystery," because they appeared so suddenly and spread so fast.

Flowers changed the face of the planet. Without them, the world we know—even man himself—would never have existed. Francis Thompson, the English poet, once wrote that one could not pluck a flower without troubling a star. Intuitively he had sensed like a naturalist the enormous interlinked complexity of life. Today we know that the appearance of the flowers contained also the equally mystifying emergence of man.

If we were to go back into the Age of Reptiles, its drowned swamps and birdless forests would reveal to us a warmer but, on the whole, a sleepier world than that of today. Here and there, it is true, the serpent heads of bottom-feeding dinosaurs might be upreared in suspicion of their huge flesh-eating compatriots. Tyrannosaurs, enormous bipedal caricatures of men, would stalk mindlessly across the sites of future cities and go their slow way down into the dark of geologic time.

In all that world of living things nothing saw save with the intense concentration of the hunt, nothing moved except with the grave sleep-walking intentness of the instinct-driven brain. Judged by modern standards, it was a world in slow motion, a cold-blooded world whose occupants were most active at noonday but torpid on chill nights, their brains damped by a slower metabolism than any known to even the most primitive of warm-blooded animals today.

A high metabolic rate and the maintenance of a constant body temperature are supreme achievements in the evolution of life. They enable an animal to escape, within broad limits, from the overheating or the chilling of its immediate surroundings, and at the same time to maintain a peak mental efficiency. Creatures without a high metabolic rate are slaves to weather. Insects in the first frosts of autumn all run down like little clocks. Yet if you pick one up and breathe warmly upon it, it will begin to move about once more.

In a sheltered spot such creatures may sleep away the winter, but they are hopelessly immobilized. Though a few warm-blooded mammals, such as the woodchuck of our day, have evolved a way of reducing their metabolic rate in order to undergo winter hibernation, it is a survival mechanism with drawbacks, for it leaves the animal helplessly exposed if enemies discover him during his period of suspended animation. Thus bear or woodchuck, big animal or small, must seek, in this time of descending sleep, a safe refuge in some hidden den or burrow. Hibernation is, therefore, primarily a winter refuge of small, easily concealed animals rather than of large ones.

A high metabolic rate, however, means a heavy intake of energy in order to sustain body warmth and efficiency. It is for this reason that even some of these later warm-blooded mammals existing in our day have learned to descend into a slower, unconscious rate of living during the winter months when food may be difficult to obtain. On a slightly higher plane they are following the procedure of the cold-blooded frog sleeping in the mud at the bottom of a frozen pond.

The agile brain of the warm-blooded birds and mammals demands a high oxygen consumption and food in concentrated forms, or the creatures cannot long sustain themselves. It was the rise of the flowering plants that provided that energy and changed the nature of the living world. Their appearance parallels in a quite surprising manner the rise of the birds and mammals.

Slowly, toward the dawn of the Age of Reptiles, something over two hundred and fifty million years ago, the little naked sperm cells wriggling their way through dew and raindrops had given way to a kind of pollen carried by the wind. Our present-day pine forests represent plants of a pollen-disseminating variety. Once fertilization was no longer dependent on exterior water, the march over drier regions could be extended. Instead of spores simple primitive seeds carrying some nourishment for the young plant had developed, but true flowers were still scores of millions of years away. After a long period of hesitant evolutionary groping, they exploded upon the world with truly revolutionary violence.

The event occurred in Cretaceous times in the close of the Age of Reptiles. Before the coming of the flowering plants our own ancestral stock, the warm-blooded mammals, consisted of a few mousy little creatures hidden in trees and underbrush. A few lizard-like birds with carnivorous teeth flapped awkwardly on ill-aimed flights among archaic shrubbery. None of these insignificant creatures gave evidence of any remarkable talents. The mammals in particular had been around for some millions of years, but had remained well lost in the shadow of the mighty reptiles. Truth to tell, man was still, like the genie in the bottle, encased in the body of a creature about the size of a rat.

As for the birds, their reptilian cousins the Pterodactyls, flew farther and better. There was just one thing about the birds that paralleled the physiology of the mammals. They, too, had evolved warm blood and its accompanying temperature control. Nevertheless, if one had been seen stripped of his feathers, he would still have seemed a slightly uncanny and unsightly lizard.

Neither the birds nor the mammals, however, were quite what they seemed. They were waiting for the Age of Flowers. They were waiting for what flowers, and with them the true encased seed, would bring. Fish-eating, gigantic leather-winged reptiles, twenty-eight feet from wing tip to wing tip, hovered over the coasts that one day would be swarming with gulls.

Inland the monotonous green of the pine and spruce forests with their primitive wooden cone flowers stretched everywhere. No grass hindered the fall of the naked seeds to earth. Great sequoias towered to the skies. The world of that time has a certain appeal but it is a giant's world, a world moving slowly like the reptiles who stalked magnificently among the boles of its trees.

The trees themselves are ancient, slow-growing and immense, like the redwood groves that have survived to our day on the California coast. All is stiff, formal, upright and green, monotonously green. There is no grass as yet; there are no wide plains rolling in the sun, no tiny daisies dotting the meadows underfoot. There is little versatility about this scene; it is, in truth, a giant's world.

A few nights ago it was brought home vividly to me that the world has changed since that far epoch. I was awakened out of sleep by an unknown sound in my living room. Not a small sound—not a creaking timber or a mouse's scurry—but a sharp, rending explosion as though an unwary foot had been put down upon a wine glass. I had come instantly out of sleep and lay tense, unbreathing. I listened for another step. There was none.

Unable to stand the suspense any longer, I turned on the light and passed from room to room glancing uneasily behind chairs and into closets. Nothing seemed disturbed, and I stood puzzled in the center of the living room floor. Then a small button-shaped object upon the rug caught my eye. It was hard and polished and glistening. Scattered over the length of the room were several more shining up at me like wary little eyes. A pine cone that had been lying in a dish had been blown the length of the coffee table. The dish itself could hardly have been the source of the explosion. Beside it I found two ribbon-like strips of a velvety-green. I tried to place the two strips together to make a pod. They twisted resolutely away from each other and would no longer fit.

I relaxed in a chair, then, for I had reached a solution of the midnight disturbance. The twisted strips were wistaria pods that I had brought in a day or two previously and placed in the dish. They had chosen midnight to explode and distribute their multiplying fund of life down the length of the room. A plant, a fixed, rooted thing, immobilized in a single spot, had devised a way of propelling its offspring across open space. Immediately there passed before my eyes the million airy troopers of the milkweed pod and the clutching hooks of the sandburs. Seeds on the coyote's tail, seeds on the hunter's coat, thistledown mounting on the winds—all were somehow triumphing over life's limitations. Yet the ability to do this had not been with them at the beginning. It was the product of endless effort and experiment.

The seeds on my carpet were not going to lie stiffly where they had dropped like their antiquated cousins, the naked seeds on the pine-cone scales. They were travelers. Struck by the thought, I went out next day and collected several other varieties. I line them up now in a row on my desk—so many little capsules of life, winged, hooked or spiked. Every one is an angiosperm, a product of the true flowering plants. Contained in these little boxes is the secret of that far-off Cretaceous explosion of a hundred million years ago that changed the face of the planet. And somewhere in here, I think, as I poke seriously at one particularly resistant seedcase of a wild grass, was once man himself.

When the first simple flower bloomed on some raw upland late in the Dinosaur Age, it was wind pollinated, just like its early pine-cone relatives. It was a very inconspicuous flower because it had not yet evolved the idea of using the surer attraction of birds and insects to achieve the transportation of pollen. It sowed its own pollen and received the pollen of other flowers by the simple vagaries of the wind. Many plants in regions where insect life is scant still follow this principle today. Nevertheless, the true flower—and the seed that it produced—was a profound innovation in the world of life.

In a way, this event parallels, in the plant world, what happened among animals. Consider the relative chance for survival of the exteriorly deposited egg of a fish in contrast with the fertilized egg of a mammal, carefully retained for months in the mother's body until the young animal (or human being) is developed to a point where it may survive. The biological wastage is less—and so it is with the flowering plants. The primitive spore, a single cell fertilized in the beginning by a swimming sperm, did not promote rapid distribution, and the young plant, moreover, had to struggle up from nothing. No one had left it any food except what it could get by its own unaided efforts.

By contrast, the true flowering plants (angiosperm itself means "encased seed") grew a seed in the heart of a flower, a seed whose development was initiated by a fertilizing pollen grain independent of outside moisture. But the seed, unlike the developing spore, is already a fully equipped *embryonic plant* packed in a little enclosed box stuffed full of nutritious food. Moreover, by featherdown attachments, as in dandelion or milkweed seed, it can be wafted upward on gusts and ride the wind for miles; or with hooks it can cling to a bear's or a rabbit's hide; or like some of the berries, it can be covered with a juicy, attractive fruit to lure birds, pass undigested through their intestinal tracts and be voided miles away.

The ramifications of this biological invention were endless. Plants traveled as they had never traveled before. They got into strange environments heretofore never entered by the old spore plants or stiff pine-cone-seed plants. The well-fed, carefully cherished little embryos raised their heads everywhere. Many of the older plants with more primitive reproductive mechanisms began to fade away under this unequal contest. They contracted their range into secluded environments. Some, like the giant redwoods, lingered on as relics; many vanished entirely.

The world of the giants was a dying world. These fantastic little seeds skipping and hopping and flying about the woods and valleys brought with them an amazing adaptability. If our whole lives had not been spent in the midst of it, it would astound us. The old, stiff, sky-reaching wooden world had changed into something that glowed here and there with strange colors, put out queer, unheard-of fruits and little intricately carved seed cases, and, most important of all, produced concentrated foods in a way that the land had never seen before, or dreamed of back in the fish-eating, leaf-crunching days of the dinosaurs.

That food came from three sources, all produced by the reproductive system of the flowering plants. There were the tantalizing nectars and pollens intended to draw insects for pollenizing purposes, and which are responsible also for that wonderful jeweled creation, the hummingbird. There were the juicy and enticing fruits to attract larger animals, and in which tough coated seeds were concealed, as in the tomato, for example. Then, as if this were not enough, there was the food in the actual seed itself, the food intended to nourish the embryo. All over the world, like hot corn in a popper, these incredible elaborations of the flowering plants kept exploding. In a movement that was almost instantaneous, geologically speaking, the angiosperms had taken over the world. Grass was beginning to cover the bare earth until, today, there are over six thousand species. All kinds of vines and bushes squirmed and writhed under new trees with flying seeds.

The explosion was having its effect on animal life also. Specialized groups of insects were arising to feed on the new sources of food and, incidentally and unknowingly, to pollinate the plant. The flowers bloomed and bloomed in ever larger and more spectacular varieties. Some were pale unearthly night flowers intended to lure moths in the evening twilight, some among the orchids even took the shape of female spiders in order to attract wandering males, some flamed redly in the light of noon or twinkled modestly in the meadow grasses. Intricate mechanisms splashed pollen on the breasts of hummingbirds, or stamped it on the bellies of black, grumbling bees droning assiduously from blossom to blossom. Honey ran, insects multiplied, and even the descendants of that toothed and ancient lizard-bird had become strangely altered. Equipped with prodding beaks instead of biting teeth they pecked the seeds and gobbled the insects that were really converted nectar.

Across the planet grasslands were now spreading. A slow continental upthrust which had been a part of the early Age of Flowers had cooled the world's climates. The stalking reptiles and the leather-winged black imps of the seashore cliffs had vanished. Only birds roamed the air now, hot-blooded and high-speed metabolic machines.

The mammals, too, had survived and were venturing into new domains, staring about perhaps a bit bewildered at their sudden eminence now that the thunder lizards were gone. Many of them, beginning as small browsers upon leaves in the forest, began to venture out upon this new sunlit world of the grass. Grass has a high silica content and demands a new type of very tough and resistant tooth enamel, but the seeds taken incidentally in the cropping of the grass are highly nutritious. A new world had opened out for the warm-blooded mammals. Great herbivores like the mammoths, horses and bisons appeared. Skulking about them had arisen savage flesh-feeding carnivores like the now extinct dire wolves and the saber-toothed tiger.

Flesh eaters though these creatures were, they were being sustained on nutritious grasses one step removed. Their fierce energy was being maintained on a high, effective level, through hot days and frosty nights, by the concentrated energy of the angiosperms. That energy, thirty percent or more of the weight of the entire plant among some of the cereal grasses, was being accumulated and concentrated in the rich proteins and fats of the enormous game herds of the grasslands.

On the edge of the forest, a strange, old-fashioned animal still hesitated. His body was the body of a tree dweller, and though tough and knotty by human standards, he was, in terms of that world into which he gazed, a weakling. His teeth, though strong for chewing on the tough fruits of the forest, or for crunching an occasional unwary bird caught with his prehensile hands, were not the tearing sabers of the great cats. He had a passion for lifting himself up to see about, in his restless, roving curiosity. He would run a little stiffly and uncertainly, perhaps, on his hind legs, but only in those rare moments when he ventured out upon the ground. All this was the legacy of his climbing days; he had a hand with flexible fingers and no fine specialized hoofs upon which to gallop like the wind.

If he had any idea of competing in that new world, he had better forget it; teeth or hooves, he was much too late for either. He was a ne'er-do-well, an in-betweener. Nature had not done well by him. It was as if she had hesitated and never quite made up her mind. Perhaps as a consequence he had a malicious gleam in his eye, the gleam of an outcast who has been left nothing and knows he is going to have to take what he gets. One day a little band of these odd apes—for apes they were—shambled out upon the grass; the human story had begun.

Apes were to become men, in the inscrutable wisdom of nature, because flowers had produced seeds and fruits in such tremendous quantities that a new and totally different store of energy had become available in concentrated form. Impressive as the slow-moving, dim-brained dinosaurs had been, it is doubtful if their age had supported anything like the diversity of life that now rioted across the planet or flashed in and out among the trees. Down on the grass by a streamside, one of those apes with inquisitive fingers turned over a stone and hefted it vaguely. The group clucked together in a throaty tongue and moved off through the tall grass foraging for seeds and insects. The one still held, sniffed, and hefted the stone he had found. He liked the feel of it in his fingers. The attack on the animal world was about to begin.

If one could run the story of that first human group like a speeded-up motion picture through a million years of time, one might see the stone in the hand change to the flint ax and the torch. All that swarming grassland world with its giant bison and trumpeting mammoths would go down in ruin to feed the insatiable and growing numbers of a carnivore who, like the great cats before him, was taking his energy indirectly from the grass. Later he found fire and it altered the tough meats and drained their energy even faster into a stomach ill adapted for the ferocious turn man's habits had taken.

His limbs grew longer, he strode more purposefully over the grass. The stolen energy that would take man across the continents would fail him at last. The great Ice Age herds were destined to vanish. When they did so, another hand like the hand that had grasped the stone by the river long ago would pluck a handful of grass seed and hold it contemplatively.

In that moment, the golden towers of man, his swarming millions, his turning wheels, the vast learning of his packed libraries, would glimmer dimly there in the ancestor of wheat, a few seeds held in a muddy hand. Without the gift of flowers and the infinite diversity of their fruits, man and bird, if they had continued to exist at all, would be today unrecognizable. Archaeopteryx, the lizard-bird, might still be snapping at beetles on a sequoia limb; man might still be a nocturnal insectivore gnawing a roach in the dark. The weight of a petal has changed the face of the world and made it ours.

The Judgment of the Birds

It is a commonplace of all religious thought, even the most primitive, that the man seeking visions and insight must go apart from his fellows and live for a time in the wilderness. If he is of the proper sort, he will return with a message. It may not be a message from the god he set out to seek, but even if he has failed in that particular, he will have had a vision or seen a marvel, and these are always worth listening to and thinking about.

The world, I have come to believe, is a very queer place, but we have been part of this queerness for so long that we tend to take it for granted. We rush to and fro like Mad Hatters upon our peculiar errands, all the time imagining our surroundings to be dull and ourselves quite ordinary creatures. Actually, there is nothing in the world to encourage this idea, but such is the mind of man, and this is why he finds it necessary from time to time to send emissaries into the wilderness in the hope of learning of great events, or plans in store for him, that will resuscitate his waning taste for life. His great news services, his world-wide radio network, he knows with a last remnant of healthy distrust will be of no use to him in this matter. No miracle can withstand a radio broadcast, and it is certain that it would be no miracle if it could. One must seek, then, what only the solitary approach can give—a natural revelation.

Let it be understood that I am not the sort of man to whom is entrusted direct knowledge of great events or prophecies. A naturalist, however, spends much of his life alone, and my life is no exception. Even in New York City there are patches of wilderness, and a man by himself is bound to undergo certain experiences falling into the class of which I speak. I set mine down, therefore: a matter of pigeons, a flight of chemicals, and a judgment of birds, in the hope that they will come to the eye of those who have retained a true taste for the marvelous, and who are capable of discerning in the flow of ordinary events the point at which the mundane world gives way to quite another dimension.

New York is not, on the whole, the best place to enjoy the downright miraculous nature of the planet. There are, I do not doubt, many remarkable stories to be heard there and many strange sights to be seen, but to grasp a marvel fully it must be savored from all aspects. This cannot be done while one is being jostled and hustled along a crowded street. Nevertheless, in any city there are true wildernesses where a man can be alone. It can happen in a hotel room, or on the high roofs at dawn.

One night on the twentieth floor of a midtown hotel I awoke in the dark and grew restless. On an impulse I climbed upon the broad old-fashioned window sill, opened the curtains and peered out. It was the hour just before dawn, the hour when men sigh in their sleep, or, if awake, strive to focus their wavering eyesight upon a world emerging from the shadows. I leaned out sleepily through the open window. I had expected depths, but not the sight I saw.

I found I was looking down from that great height into a series of curious cupolas or lofts that I could just barely make out in the darkness. As I looked, the outlines of these lofts became more distinct because the light was being reflected from the wings of pigeons who, in utter silence, were beginning to float outward upon the city. In and out through the open slits in the cupolas passed the white-winged birds on their mysterious errands. At this hour the city was theirs, and quietly, without the brush of a single wing tip against stone in that high, eerie place, they were taking over the spires of Manhattan. They were pouring upward in a light that was not yet perceptible to human eyes, while far down in the black darkness of the alleys it was still midnight.

As I crouched half asleep across the sill, I had a moment's illusion that the world had changed in the night, as in some immense snowfall, and that if I were to leave, it would have to be as these other inhabitants were doing, by the window. I should have to launch out into that great bottomless void with the simple confidence of young birds reared high up there among the familiar chimney pots and interposed horrors of the abyss.

I leaned farther out. To and fro went the white wings, to and fro. There were no sounds from any of them. They knew man was asleep and this light for a little while was theirs. Or perhaps I had only dreamed about man in this city of wings—which he could surely never have built. Perhaps I, myself, was one of these birds dreaming unpleasantly a moment of old dangers far below as I teetered on a window ledge.

Around and around went the wings. It needed only a little courage, only a little shove from the window ledge to enter that city of light. The muscles of my hands were already making little premonitory lunges. I wanted to enter that city and go away over the roofs in the first dawn. I wanted to enter it so badly that I drew back carefully into the room and opened the hall door. I found my coat on the chair, and it slowly became clear to me that there was a way down through the floors, that I was, after all, only a man.

I dressed then and went back to my own kind, and I have been rather more than usually careful ever since not to look into the city of light. I had seen, just once, man's greatest creation from a strange inverted angle, and it was not really his at all. I will never forget how those wings went round and round, and how, by the merest pressure of the fingers and a feeling for air, one might go away over the roofs. It is a knowledge, however, that is better kept to oneself. I think of it sometimes in such a way that the wings, beginning far down in the black depths of the mind, begin to rise and whirl till all the mind is lit by their spinning, and there is a sense of things passing away, but lightly, as a wing might veer over an obstacle.

To see from an inverted angle, however, is not a gift allotted merely to the human imagination. I have come to suspect that within their degree it is sensed by animals, though perhaps as rarely as among men. The time has to be right; one has to be, by chance or intention, upon the border of two worlds. And sometimes these two borders may shift or interpenetrate and one sees the miraculous.

I once saw this happen to a crow.

This crow lives near my house, and though I have never injured him, he takes good care to stay up in the very highest trees and, in general, to avoid humanity. His world begins at about the limit of my eyesight.

On the particular morning when this episode occurred, the whole countryside was buried in one of the thickest fogs in years. The ceiling was absolutely zero. All planes were grounded, and even a pedestrian could hardly see his outstretched hand before him.

I was groping across a field in the general direction of the railroad station, following a dimly outlined path. Suddenly out of the fog, at about the level of my eyes, and so closely that I flinched, there flashed a pair of immense black wings and a huge beak. The whole bird rushed over my head with a frantic cawing outcry of such hideous terror as I have never heard in a crow's voice before, and never expect to hear again.

He was lost and startled, I thought, as I recovered my poise. He ought not to have flown out in this fog. He'd knock his silly brains out.

All afternoon that great awkward cry rang in my head. Merely being lost in a fog seemed scarcely to account for it—especially in a tough, intelligent old bandit such as I knew that particular crow to be. I even looked once in the mirror to see what it might be about me that had so revolted him that he had cried out in protest to the very stones.

Finally, as I worked my way homeward along the path, the solution came to me. It should have been clear before. The borders of our worlds had shifted. It was the fog that had done it. That crow, and I knew him well, never under normal circumstances flew low near men. He had been lost all right, but it was more than that. He had thought he was high up, and when he encountered me looming gigantically through the fog, he had perceived a ghastly and, to the crow mind, unnatural sight. He had seen a man walking on air, desecrating the very heart of the crow kingdom, a harbinger of the most profound evil a crow mind could conceive of—air-walking men. The encounter, he must have thought, had taken place a hundred feet over the roofs.

He caws now when he sees me leaving for the station in the morning, and I fancy that in that note I catch the uncertainty of a mind that has come to know things are not always what they seem. He has seen a marvel in his heights of air and is no longer as other crows. He has experienced the human world from an unlikely perspective. He and I share a viewpoint in common: our worlds have interpenetrated, and we both have faith in the miraculous.

It is a faith that in my own case has been augmented by two remarkable sights. As I have hinted previously, I once saw some very odd chemicals fly across a waste so dead it might have been upon the moon, and once, by an even more fantastic piece of luck, I was present when a group of birds passed a judgment upon life.

On the maps of the old voyageurs it is called *Mauvaises Terres,* the evil lands, and, slurred a little with the passage through many minds, it has come down to us anglicized as the Badlands. The soft shuffle of moccasins has passed through its canyons on the grim business of war and flight, but the last of those slight disturbances of immemorial silences died out almost a century ago. The land, if one can call it a land, is a waste as lifeless as that valley in which lie the kings of Egypt. Like the Valley of the Kings, it is a mausoleum, a place of dry bones in what once was a place of life. Now it has silences as deep as those in the moon's airless chasms.

Nothing grows among its pinnacles; there is no shade except under great toadstools of sandstone whose bases have been eaten to the shape of wine glasses by the wind. Everything is flaking, cracking, disintegrating, wearing away in the long, imperceptible weather of time. The ash of ancient volcanic outbursts still sterilizes its soil, and its colors in that waste are the colors that flame in the lonely sunsets on dead planets. Men come there but rarely, and for one purpose only, the collection of bones.

It was a late hour on a cold, wind-bitten autumn day when I climbed a great hill spined like a dinosaur's back and tried to take my bearings. The tumbled waste fell away in waves in all directions. Blue air was darkening into purple along the bases of the hills. I shifted my knapsack, heavy with the petrified bones of long-vanished creatures, and studied my compass. I wanted to be out of there by nightfall, and already the sun was going sullenly down in the west.

It was then that I saw the flight coming on. It was moving like a little close-knit body of black specks that danced and darted and closed again. It was pouring from the north and heading toward me with the undeviating relentlessness of a compass needle. It streamed through the shadows rising out of monstrous gorges. It rushed over towering pinnacles in the red light of the sun, or momentarily sank from sight within their shade. Across that desert of eroding clay and wind-worn stone they came with a faint wild twittering that filled all the air about me as those tiny living bullets hurtled past into the night.

It may not strike you as a marvel. It would not, perhaps, unless you stood in the middle of a dead world at sunset, but that was where I stood. Fifty million years lay under my feet, fifty million years of bellowing monsters moving in a green world now gone so utterly that its very light was traveling on the farther edge of space. The chemicals of all that vanished age lay about me in the ground. Around me still lay the shearing molars of dead titanotheres, the delicate sabers of soft-stepping cats, the hollow sockets that had held the eyes of many a strange, outmoded beast. Those eyes had looked out upon a world as real as ours; dark, savage brains had roamed and roared their challenges into the steaming night.

Now they were still here, or, put it as you will, the chemicals that made them were here about me in the ground. The carbon that had driven them ran blackly in the eroding stone. The stain of iron was in the clays. The iron did not remember the blood it had once moved within, the phosphorus had forgot the savage brain. The little individual moment had ebbed from all those strange combinations of chemicals as it would ebb from our living bodies into the sinks and runnels of oncoming time.

I had lifted up a fistful of that ground. I held it while that wild flight of south-bound warblers hurtled over me into the oncoming dark. There went phosphorus, there went iron, there went carbon, there beat the calcium in those hurrying wings. Alone on a dead planet I watched that incredible miracle speeding past. It ran by some true compass over field and wasteland. It cried its individual ecstasies into the air until the gullies rang. It swerved like a single body, it knew itself and, lonely, it bunched close in the racing darkness, its individual entities feeling about them the rising night. And so, crying to each other their identity, they passed away out of my view.

I dropped my fistful of earth. I heard it roll inanimate back into the gully at the base of the hill: iron, carbon, the chemicals of life. Like men from those wild tribes who had haunted these hills before me seeking visions, I made my sign to the great darkness. It was not a mocking sign, and I was not mocked. As I walked into my camp late that night, one man, rousing from his blankets beside the fire, asked sleepily, "What did you see?"

"I think, a miracle," I said softly, but I said it to myself. Behind me that vast waste began to glow under the rising moon.

I have said that I saw a judgment upon life, and that it was not passed by men. Those who stare at birds in cages or who test minds by their closeness to our own may not care for it. It comes from far away out of my past, in a place of pouring waters and green leaves. I shall never see an episode like it again if I live to be a hundred, nor do I think that one man in a million has ever seen it, because man is an intruder into such silences. The light must be right, and the observer must remain unseen. No man sets up such an experiment. What he sees, he sees by chance.

You may put it that I had come over a mountain, that I had slogged through fern and pine needles for half a long day, and that on the edge of a little glade with one long, crooked branch extending across it, I had sat down to rest with my back against a stump. Through accident I was concealed from the glade, although I could see into it perfectly.

The sun was warm there, and the murmurs of forest life blurred softly away into my sleep. When I awoke, dimly aware of some commotion and outcry in the clearing, the light was slanting down through the pines in such a way that the glade was lit like some vast cathedral. I could see the dust motes of wood pollen in the long shaft of light, and there on the extended branch sat an enormous raven with a red and squirming nestling in his beak.

The sound that awoke me was the outraged cries of the nestling's parents, who flew helplessly in circles about the clearing. The sleek black monster was indifferent to them. He gulped, whetted his beak on the dead branch a moment and sat still. Up to that point the little tragedy had followed the usual pattern. But suddenly, out of all that area of woodland, a soft sound of complaint began to rise. Into the glade fluttered small birds of half a dozen varieties drawn by the anguished outcries of the tiny parents.

No one dared to attack the raven. But they cried there in some instinctive common misery, the bereaved and the unbereaved. The glade filled with their soft rustling and their cries. They fluttered as though to point their wings at the murderer. There was a dim intangible ethic he had violated, that they knew. He was a bird of death.

And he, the murderer, the black bird at the heart of life, sat on there, glistening in the common light, formidable, unmoving, unperturbed, untouchable.

The sighing died. It was then I saw the judgment. It was the judgment of life against death. I will never see it again so forcefully presented. I will never hear it again in notes so tragically prolonged. For in the midst of protest, they forgot the violence. There, in that clearing, the crystal note of a song sparrow lifted hesitantly in the hush. And finally, after painful fluttering, another took the song, and then another, the song passing from one bird to another, doubtfully at first, as though some evil thing were being slowly forgotten. Till suddenly they took heart and sang from many throats joyously together as birds are known to sing. They sang because life is sweet and sunlight beautiful. They sang under the brooding shadow of the raven. In simple truth they had forgotten the raven, for they were the singers of life, and not of death.

I was not of that airy company. My limbs were the heavy limbs of an earthbound creature who could climb mountains, even the mountains of the mind, only by a great effort of will. I knew I had seen a marvel and observed a judgment, but the mind which was my human endowment was sure to question it and to be at me day by day with its heresies until I grew to doubt the meaning of what I had seen. Eventually darkness and subtleties would ring me round once more.

And so it proved until, on the top of a stepladder, I made one more observation upon life. It was cold that autumn evening, and, standing under a suburban streetlight in a spate of leaves and beginning snow,

I was suddenly conscious of some huge and hairy shadows dancing over the pavement. They seemed attached to an odd, globular shape that was magnified above me. There was no mistaking it. I was standing under the shadow of an orb-weaving spider. Gigantically projected against the street, she was about her spinning when everything was going underground. Even her cables were magnified upon the sidewalk and already I was half-entangled in their shadows.

"Good Lord," I thought, "she has found herself a kind of minor sun and is going to upset the course of nature."

I procured a ladder from my yard and climbed up to inspect the situation. There she was, the universe running down around her, warmly arranged among her guy ropes attached to the lamp supports—a great black and yellow embodiment of the life force, not giving up to either frost or stepladders. She ignored me and went on tightening and improving her web.

I stood over her on the ladder, a faint snow touching my cheeks, and surveyed her universe. There were a couple of iridescent green beetle cases turning slowly on a loose strand of web, a fragment of luminescent eye from a moth's wing and a large indeterminable object, perhaps a cicada, that had struggled and been wrapped in silk. There were also little bits and slivers, little red and blue flashes from the scales of anonymous wings that had crashed there.

Some days, I thought, they will be dull and gray and the shine will be out of them; then the dew will polish them again and drops hang on the silk until everything is gleaming and turning in the light. It is like a mind, really, where everything changes but remains, and in the end you have these eaten-out bits of experience like beetle wings.

I stood over her a moment longer, comprehending somewhat reluctantly that her adventure against the great blind forces of winter, her seizure of this warming globe of light, would come to nothing and was hopeless. Nevertheless it brought the birds back into mind, and that faraway song which had traveled with growing strength around a forest clearing years ago—a kind of heroism, a world where even a spider refuses to lie down and die if a rope can still be spun on to a star. Maybe man himself will fight like this in the end, I thought, slowly realizing that the web and its threatening yellow occupant had been added to some luminous store of experience, shining for a moment in the fogbound reaches of my brain.

The mind, it came to me as I slowly descended the ladder, is a very remarkable thing; it has gotten itself a kind of courage by looking at a spider in a street lamp. Here was something that ought to be passed on to those who will fight our final freezing battle with the void. I thought of setting it down carefully as a message to the future: *In the days of the frost seek a minor sun.*

But as I hesitated, it became plain that something was wrong. The marvel was escaping—a sense of bigness beyond man's power to grasp, the essence of life in its great dealings with the universe. It was better, I decided, for the emissaries returning from the wilderness, even if they were merely descending from a stepladder, to record their marvel, not to define its meaning. In that way it would go echoing on through the minds of men, each grasping at that beyond out of which the miracles emerge, and which, once defined, ceases to satisfy the human need for symbols.

In the end I merely made a mental note: One specimen of Epeira observed building a web in a street light. Late autumn and cold for spiders. Cold for men, too. I shivered and left the lamp glowing there in my mind. The last I saw of Epeira she was hauling steadily on a cable. I stepped carefully over her shadow as I walked away.

The Innocent Assassins

Once in the sun-fierce badlands of the west
in that strange country of volcanic ash and cones,
runneled by rains, cut into purgatorial shapes,
where nothing grows, no seeds spring, no beast moves,
we found a sabertooth, most ancient cat,
far down in all those cellars of dead time.
What was it made the mystery there? We dug
until the full length of the striking saber showed
beautiful as Toledo steel, the fine serrations still
present along the blade, a masterpiece of murderous art conceived
by those same forces that heaved mountains up
from the flat bottoms of Cretaceous seas.

Attentive in a little silent group we squatted there.
This was no ordinary death, though forty million years
lay between us and that most gaping snarl.
Deep-driven to the root a fractured scapula
hung on the mighty saber undetached; two beasts
had died in mortal combat, for the bone
had never been released; there was no chance
this cat had ever used its fangs again or eaten—
died there, in short, though others of its kind

grew larger, larger, suddenly were gone
while the great darkness went about its task,
mountains thrust up, mountains worn down,
till this lost battle was exposed to eyes
the stalking sabertooths had never seen.

Pure nature had devised such weapons, struck
deep in the night, endured immortally
death, ambush, terror, by these, her innocents
whose lives revolved on this, whose brains were formed
only to strike and strike, beget their kind, and go to strike again.

There were the great teeth snarling in the clay, the bony crests
that had once held the muscles for this deed,
                              perfect as yesterday.
I looked a little while, admiring how
            that marvelous weapon had been so designed
in unknown darkness, where the genes create
                              as if they planned it so.
                  I wondered why
such perfect fury had been swept away, while man,
                  wide-roaming dark assassin of his kind,
                  had sprung up in the wake
                  of such perfected instruments as these.
They lived long eras out, while we
            in all this newborn world of our own violence show
uncertainties, and hopes unfostered when
the cat's sheer leap wrenched with his killing skill
            his very self from life.
On these lost hills that mark the rise of brain,
            I weep perversely for the beauty gone.

I weep for man who knows this antique trade
    but is not guiltless
    is not born with fangs,
     has doubts,
   suppresses them as though he knew
nature had other thoughts, inchoate, dim,
but that the grandeur of great cats attracted him—
envy, perhaps, by a weak creature forced to borrow
tools from the earth, growing, in them, most cunning
    upon an outworn path.

I see us still upon that hilltop, gathered like ancient men
    who, weaponless, detach
from an old weathered skull a blade whose form reshaped in flint
could lift death up from earth's inanimate core
and hurl it at the heart. Whatever else would bring
    cold scientist to murmur over what they saw?
    We are all atavists and yet sometimes we seem
wrapped in wild innocence like sabertooths, as if we still might seek
    a road unchosen yet, another dream.

Reflections of a Writer

The Gold Wheel

In the waste fields strung with barbed wire where the thistles grow over hidden mine fields there exists a curious freedom. Between the guns of the deployed powers, between the march of patrols and policing dogs there is an uncultivated strip of land from which law and man himself have retreated. Along this uneasy border the old life of the wild has come back into its own. Weeds grow and animals slip about in the night where no man dares to hunt them. A thin uncertain line fringes the edge of oppression. The freedom it contains is fit only for birds and floating thistledown or a wandering fox. Nevertheless there must be men who look upon it with envy.

The imagination can grasp this faint underscoring of freedom but there are few who realize that precisely similar lines run in a delicate tracery along every civilized road in the West, or that these hedges of thorn apple and osage orange are the last refuge of wild life between the cultivated fields of civilization. It takes a refugee at heart, a wistful glancer over fences, to sense this one dimensional world, but it is there. I can attest to it for I myself am such a fugitive.

This confession need alarm no one. I am relatively harmless. I have not broken or entered, or passed illegally over boundaries. I am not on the lists of the police. The only time that I have gazed into the wrong end of a gun I have been the injured party. Even this episode, however, took place many years ago and was in another country at the hands of foreigners. In spite of this, I repeat that I am a fugitive. I was born one.

The world will say that this is impossible, that fugitives are made by laws and acts of violence, that without these preliminaries no man can be called a fugitive, that without pursuit no man can be hunted. It may be so. Nevertheless I know that there are men born to hunt and some few born to flee, whether physically or mentally makes no difference. That is purely a legal quibble. The fact that I wear the protective coloration of sedate citizenship is a ruse of the fox—I learned it long ago. The facts of my inner life are quite otherwise. Early, very early, the consciousness of this differences emerges. This is how it began for me.

It begins in the echoing loneliness of a house with no other children; in the silence of a deafened mother; in the child head growing strangely aware of itself as it prattled over immense and solitary games. The child learned that there were shadows in the closets and a green darkness behind the close-drawn curtains of the parlor; he was aware of a cool twilight in the basement. He was afraid only of noise.

Noise is the Outside—the bully in the next block by whose house you had to pass in order to go to school. Noise is all the things you did not wish to do. It is the games in which you were pummeled by other children's big brothers, it is the sharp, demanding voices of adults who snatch your books. Noise is day. And out of that intolerable sunlight your one purpose has been given—to escape. Few men have such motivations in childhood, few are so constantly seeking for the loophole in the fern where the leaves swing shut behind them. But I anticipate. It is in the mind that the flight commences. It is there that the arc lights lay their shadows. It is there, down those streets past unlit houses that the child runs on alone.

II

We stood in a wide flat field at sunset. For the life of me I can remember no other children before them. I must have run away and been playing by myself until I had wandered to the edge of the town. They were older than I and knew where they came from and how to get back. I joined them.

They were not going home. They were going to a place called Green Gulch. They came from some other part of town, and their clothes were rough, their eyes worldly and sly. I think, looking back, that it must have been a little like a child following goblins home to their hill at nightfall, but nobody threatened me. Besides, I was very small and did not know the way home, so I followed them.

Presently we came to some rocks. The place was well named. It was a huge pool in a sandstone basin, green and dark with the evening over it and the trees leaning secretly inward above the water. When you looked down, you saw the sky. I remember that place as it was when we came there. I remember the quiet and the green ferns touching the green water. I remember we played there, innocently at first.

But someone found the spirit of the place, a huge old turtle, asleep in the ferns. He was the last lord of the green water before the town poured over it. I saw his end. They pounded him to death with stones on the other side of the pool while I looked on in stupefied horror. I had never seen death before.

Suddenly, as I stood there small and uncertain and frightened, a grimy, splattered gnome who had been stooping over the turtle stood up with a rock in his hand. He looked at me, and around that little group some curious evil impulse passed like a wave. I felt it and drew back. I was alone there. They were not human.

I do not know who threw the first stone, who splashed water over my suit, who struck me first, or even who finally, among that ring of vicious faces, put me on my feet, dragged me to the roadside, pointed and said, roughly, "There's your road, kid, follow the street lamps. They'll take you home."

They stood in a little group watching me, nervous now, ashamed a little at the ferocious pack impulse toward the outsider that had swept over them.

I never forgot that moment.

I went because I had to, down that road with the wind moving in the fields. I went slowly from one spot of light to another and in between I thought the things a child thinks, so that I did not stop at any house nor ask anyone to help me when I came to the lighted streets.

I had discovered evil. It was a monstrous and corroding knowledge. It could not be told to adults because it was the evil of childhood in which no one believes. I was alone with it in the dark. And in the dark henceforth, in some fashion, I was destined to stay until, two years later, I found the gold wheel. I played alone in those days, particularly after my rejection by the boys who regarded Green Gulch as their territory. I took to creeping up alleys and peering through hedges. I was not miserable. There was a wonderful compensating secrecy about these activities. I had little shelters in hedgerows and I knew and perfected secret entrances and exits into the most amazing worlds.

There was, for example, the Rudd mansion. I never saw the inside of it, but I made the discovery that in a stone incinerator, back of the house and close up to the immense hedge through which I had worked a passage, there were often burned toys. Apparently the Rudd family lived with great prodigality and cast recklessly away what to me were invaluable possessions. I got in the habit of creeping through the hedge at nightfall and scratching in the ashes for bits of Meccano sets and other little treasures which I would bear homeward.

One frosty night in early fall I turned up a gold wheel. It was not gold really, but I pretended it was. To me it represented all those things—perhaps in a dim way life itself—that are denied by poverty. The wheel had been part of a child's construction set of some sort. It was grooved to run on a track and it had a screw on the hub to enable it to be fitted adjustably to an axle. The amalgam of which it was made was hard and golden and it had come untouched through the incinerator fires. In my childish world it was a wonderful object and I haunted the incinerator for many nights thereafter hoping I might secure the remaining wheel. The flow of toys declined, however, and I never found the second gold wheel. The one I had found became a sort of fetish which I carried around with me. I had become very conscious of gold wheels and finally I made up my mind to run away upon a pair of them.

My decision came about through the appearance in our neighborhood of a tea wagon which used to stop once or twice a week at the house next door. This was not an ordinary delivery wagon. It was a neatly enclosed cart and at the rear beneath a latched door was a little step for the convenience of the driver when he wished to come around in back and secure the packages of tea which he sold.

Two things occupied my attention at once. First, the little footboard was of just the right height and size to permit a small boy to sit upon it and ride away unseen once the driver had taken the reins and seated himself at the front of the cart. In addition, the wheels of the cart were large and long-spoked and painted a bright golden yellow. When the horse broke into a spanking trot those wheels spun and glittered in the equally golden air of autumn with an irresistible attraction. Upon that rear step I had made my decision to launch out into the world. It was not the product of a momentary whim. I studied for several days the habits of the tea man until I knew the moment to run forward and perch upon the step. It never crossed my mind to concern myself with where he was going. Such adults matters happily never troubled me. It was enough to be gone between a pair of spinning golden wheels.

On the appointed day, without provision for the future and with a renewed sublime trust in the permanence of sunshine and all good and golden things, I essayed my first great venture into the outer wilderness. My mother was busy with her dishes in the kitchen. As the tea wagon drew up to the house next door I loitered by a bush in the front yard. When the driver leapt once more upon his box I swung hastily upon the little step at the rear. There was no flaw in my escape. The horse trotted with increasing speed over the cobbles, the wheels spun on either side of me in the sunshine, and I was off through the city traffic, followed by the amused or concerned stares of adults along the street. I jounced and bumped but my hold was secure. Horseshoes rang and the whole bright world was one glitter of revolving gold. I had never clearly dealt with the problem of what I would do if the driver continued to make stops, but now it appeared such fears were groundless. There were no more stops. The wheels spun faster and faster. We were headed for the open countryside.

It was, I think, the most marvelous ride I shall ever make in this life. I can still hear the pounding echo of the horse's hoofs over wooden bridges. Shafts of light—it was growing cloudy now—moved over the green meadows by the roadside. I have traversed that road many times since, but the green is faded, the flowers ordinary. On that day, however, we were moving through the kind of eternal light which exists only in the minds of the very young. I remember one other queer thing about the journey: the driver made no impression on my mind at all. I do not recall a cry, a crack of the whip, anything to indicate his genuine presence. We went clopping steadily down a long hill, and up, up against the sky where black clouds were beginning to boil and billow with the threat of an oncoming storm. Far up on that great hill I had a momentary flash of memory. We were headed for the bishop's house.

The bishop's house, which lay thus well out into the country beside an orphanage, was a huge place of massive stone so well set and timeless that it gave the appearance of having been there before the city was built. I had heard my elders speak of it with a touch of awe in their voices. It had high battlements of red granite and around the yard ran a black iron fence through which, according to story, only the baptised might pass. Inside, accepted by my childish mind, was another somewhat supernatural world shut off by hedges.

As we wound higher along the skyline I could see the ruts in the road wriggle, diverge, and merge beneath my dangling feet. Because of my position at the rear of the cart it was impossible to see ahead. The first drops of rain were beginning to make little puffs of dirt in the road and finally as we slowed to a walk on the drive leading up to the gates the storm caught up to us in a great gust of wind and driving rain.

With scarce a pause the iron gates swung open for the tea wagon. I heard the horseshoes ringing on the stones of the drive as I leaped from my perch on the little step and darted into the safety of the hedge. The thunder from the clouds mingled with the hollow rolling of the wheels and the crash of the closing gates before me echoed through my frightened head with a kind of dreadful finality. It was only then, in the intermittent flashes of the lightning, that I realized I was not alone.

In the hedge where I crouched beside the bishop's gate were many hundreds of brown birds, strangers, sitting immovable and still. They paid no attention to me. In fact, they were immersed in a kind of waiting silence so secret and immense that I was much too overawed to disturb them. Instead, I huddled into this thin world beneath the birds while the storm leaped and flickered as though hesitating whether to harry us out of our refuge into the rolling domain of the clouds. Today I know that those birds were migrating and had sought shelter from exhaustion. On that desolate countryside they had come unerringly down upon the thin line of the bishop's hedge.

The tea wagon had unaccountably vanished. The storm after a time grumbled its way slowly into the distance and with equal slowness I crept unwillingly out onto the wet road and began my long walk homeward. I felt in the process some obscure sense of loss. It was as though I had been on the verge of a great adventure into another world that had eluded me; the green light had passed away from the fields. I thought once wistfully of the gold wheel I had failed to find and that seemed vaguely linked to my predicament. I was destined to see it only once in the years that followed—those mature years in which, slower and slower, dimmer and dimmer, the fancies and passions of childhood fade away into the past. Strangely enough, it returned in a moment of violence.

III

The event was simple. There were three of us, jammed into the seat of a stripped car. We were doing fifty miles an hour over a stretch of open grassland, while ahead of us still flashed the white hindquarters of a running antelope. There was no road; no signs, no warnings. There was only the green fenceless unrolling plain and that elusive steel-hearted beast dancing away before us.

The driver pushed the pedal toward the floor.

"You can kill him from here," he said and gestured toward the rifle on my lap.

I did not want to kill him. I looked for a barrier, a fence, an obstacle to wheels, something to stop this game while it was still fun. I wanted to see that unscathed animal go over a hedge and vanish, leaving maybe a little wisp of fur on a thorn to let us know he had passed unharmed out of our reach.

I shrugged and said carefully, indifferently, for I knew the man I rode with, "Why hurry? We'll get him all right in the end."

The driver grunted and started to shift his weight once more upon the pedal. It was just then, in one final brake-screaming instant, that I saw the barrier. It was there and our beast had already cleared it without changing his stride. It was the barrier between life and death.

There was a gulch five feet wide and maybe eight feet deep coming up to meet us, its edge well hidden in the prairie grass. As we saw it we struck, the front wheels colliding and exploding against the opposite bank. By some freak of pressures we remained there stunned, the bumper holding us above the pit. In that moment, as my head snapped nearly into blackness, I saw a loose golden wheel rolling and rolling on the prairie grass. In my ears resounded the thunder of the tea wagon pounding over the cobbles and the clank of the bishop's iron gate in the midst of the storm. Then the rumbling receded into the distance and I wiped the blood from my nose.

"He's gone," someone said stupidly.

I put my hands against the bent dashboard and shook my head to clear it.

"The man with the tea wagon?" I asked before I thought.

"The buck," someone answered a long way off, his voice a little thickened. "That buck stepped across the ravine like it wasn't there. We damn near stopped for good. It's like an invisible wall, a line you can't see."

"Yes," I said.

But I didn't say I had wished for it. I didn't say that I remembered how the birds sit on those lines and you never knew which side the birds were on because they sat so quietly and were waiting. You had to be a fugitive to know this and to know the lines were everywhere— a net running through one's brain as well as the outside world. Someday I would pass through the leaves into the open when I should have stayed under the hedge with the birds.

With an effort I lifted the rifle and climbed stiffly out, looking all around the horizon like a hunter. I wear, you see, the protective coloring of men. It is a ruse of the fox—I learned it long ago.

The Running Man

While I endured the months in the Colorado cabin, my mother, who had been offered a safe refuge in the home of her sister, quarreled and fought with everyone. Finally, in her own inelegant way of putting things, she had "skipped town" to work as a seamstress, domestic, or housekeeper upon farms. She was stone deaf. I admired her courage, but I also knew by then that she was paranoid, neurotic and unstable. What ensued on these various short-lived adventures I neither know to this day, nor wish to know.

It comes to me now in retrospect that I never saw my mother weep; it was her gift to make others suffer instead. She was an untutored, talented artist and she left me, if anything, a capacity for tremendous visual impressions just as my father, a one-time itinerant actor, had in that silenced household of the stone age—a house of gestures, of day-long facial contortion—produced for me the miracle of words when he came home. My mother had once been very beautiful. It is only thus that I can explain the fatal attraction that produced me. I have never known how my parents chanced to meet.

There will be those to say, in this mother-worshipping culture, that I am harsh, embittered. They will be quite wrong. Why should I be embittered? It is far too late. A month ago, after a passage of many years, I stood above her grave in a place called Wyuka. We, she and I, were close to being one now, lying like the skeletons of last year's leaves in a fence corner. And it was all nothing. Nothing, do you understand? All the pain, all the anguish. Nothing. We were, both of us, merely the debris life always leaves in its passing, like the maimed, discarded chicks in the hatchery trays—no more than that. For a little longer I would see and hear, but it was nothing, and to the world it would mean nothing.

I murmured to myself and tried to tell her this belatedly: Nothing, mama, nothing. Rest. You could never rest. That was your burden. But now, sleep. Soon I will join you, although, forgive me, not here. Neither of us then would rest. I will go far to lie down; the time draws on; it is unlikely that I will return. Now you will understand, I said, touching the October warmth of the gravestone. It was for nothing. It has taken me all my life to grasp this one fact.

I am, it is true, wandering out of time and place. This narrative is faltering. To tell the story of a life one is bound to linger above gravestones where memory blurs and doors can be pushed ajar, but never opened. Listen, or do not listen, it is all the same.

I am every man and no man, and will be so to the end. This is why I must tell the story as I may. Not for the nameless name upon the page, not for the trails behind me that faded or led nowhere, not for the rooms at nightfall where I slept from exhaustion or did not sleep at all, not for the confusion of where I was to go, or if I had a destiny recognizable by any star. No, in retrospect it was the loneliness of not knowing, not knowing at all.

I was a child of the early century, American man, if the term may still be tolerated. A creature molded of plains' dust and the seed of those who came west with the wagons. The names Corey, Hollister, Appleton, McKee lie strewn in graveyards from New England to the broken sticks that rotted quickly on the Oregon trail. That ancient contingent, with a lost memory and a gene or two from the Indian, is underscored by the final German of my own name.

How, among all these wanderers, should I have absorbed a code by which to live? How should I have answered in turn to the restrained Puritan, and the long hatred of the beaten hunters? How should I have curbed the flaring rages of my maternal grandfather? How should—

But this I remember out of deepest childhood—I remember the mad Shepards as I heard the name whispered among my mother's people. I remember the pacing, the endless pacing of my parents after midnight, while I lay shivering in the cold bed and tried to understand the words that passed between my mother and my father.

Once, a small toddler, I climbed from bed and seized their hands, pleading wordlessly for sleep, for peace, peace. And surprisingly they relented, even my unfortunate mother. Terror, anxiety, ostracism, shame; I did not understand the words. I learned only the feelings they represent. I repeat, I am an American whose profession, even his life, is no more than a gambler's throw by the firelight of a western wagon.

What have I to do with the city in which I live? Why, far to the west, does my mind still leap to great windswept vistas of grass or the eternal snows of the Cascades? Why does the sight of wolves in cages cause me to avert my eyes?

I will tell you only because something like this was at war in the heart of every American at the final closing of the westward trails. One of the most vivid memories I retain from my young manhood is of the wagon ruts of the Oregon trail still visible on the unplowed short-grass prairie. They stretched half a mile in width and that was only yesterday. In his young years, my own father had carried a gun and remembered the gamblers at the green tables in the cow towns. I dream inexplicably at times of a gathering of wagons, of women in sunbonnets and black-garbed, bewhiskered men. Then I wake and the scene dissolves.

I have strayed from the Shepards. It was a name to fear but this I did not learn for a long time. I thought they were the people pictured in the family Bible, men with white beards and long crooks with which they guided sheep.

In the house, when my father was away and my mother's people came to visit, the Shepards were spoken of in whispers. They were the mad Shepards, I slowly gathered, and they lay somewhere in my line of descent. When I was recalcitrant the Shepards were spoken of and linked with my name.

In that house there was no peace, yet we loved each other fiercely. Perhaps the adults were so far on into the midcountry that mistakes were never rectifiable, flight disreputable. We were Americans of the middle border where the East was forgotten and the one great western road no longer crawled with wagons.

A silence had fallen. I was one of those born into that silence. The bison had perished; the Sioux no longer rode. Only the yellow dust of the cyclonic twisters still marched across the landscape. I knew the taste of that dust in my youth. I knew it in the days of the dust bowl. No matter how far I travel it will be a fading memory upon my tongue in the hour of my death. It is the taste of one dust only, the dust of a receding ice age.

So much for my mother, the mad Shepards, and the land, but this is not all, certainly not. Some say a child's basic character is formed by the time he is five. I can believe it, I who begged for peace at four and was never blessed for long by its presence.

The late W. H. Auden once said to me over a lonely little dinner in New York before he left America, "What public event do you remember first from childhood?" I suppose the massive old lion was in his way encouraging a shy man to speak. Being of the same age we concentrated heavily upon the subject.

"I think for me, the Titanic disaster," he ventured thoughtfully.

"Of course," I said. "That would be 1912. She was a British ship and you British have always been a sea people."

"And you?" he questioned, holding me with his seamed features that always gave him the aspect of a seer.

I dropped my gaze. Was it 1914? Was it Pancho Villa's raid into New

Mexico in 1916? All westerners remembered that. We wandered momentarily among dead men and long-vanished events. Auden waited patiently.

"Well," I ventured, for it was a long-held personal secret, "It was an escape, just an escape from prison."

"Your own?" Auden asked with a trace of humor.

"No," I began, "it was the same year as the Titanic sinking. He blew the gates with nitroglycerin. I was five years old, like you." Then I paused, considering the time. "You are right," I admitted hesitantly. "I was already old enough to know one should flee from the universe but I did not know where to run." I identified with the man as I always had across the years. "We never made it," I added glumly, and shrugged. "You see, there was a warden, a prison, and a blizzard. Also there was an armed posse and a death." I could feel the same snow driving beside the window in New York. "We never made it," I repeated unconsciously.

Auden sighed and looked curiously at me. I knew he was examining the pronoun. "There are other things that constitute a child," I added hastily. "Sandpiles, for example. There was a lot of building being done then on our street. I used to spend hours turning over the gravel. Why, I wouldn't know. Finally I had a box of pretty stones and some fossils. I prospected for hours alone. It was like today in book stores, old book stores," I protested defensively.

Auden nodded in sympathy.

"I still can't tell what started it," I went on. "I was groping, I think, childishly into time, into the universe. It was to be my profession but I never understood in the least, not till much later. No other child on the block wasted his time like that. I have never understood my precise motivation, never. For actually I was retarded in the reading of clock time. Was it because, in the things found in the sand, I was already lost and wandering instinctively—amidst the debris of vanished eras?"

"Ah," Auden said kindly, "who knows these things?"

"Then there was the period of the gold crosses," I added. "Later, in another house, I had found a little bottle of liquid gilt my mother used on picture frames. I made some crosses, carefully whittled out of wood, and gilded them till they were gold. Then I placed them over an occasional dead bird I buried. Or, if I read of a tragic, heroic death like those of the war aces, I would put the clipping—I could read by then—into a little box and bury it with a gold cross to mark the spot. One day a mower in the empty lot beyond our backyard found the little cemetery and carried away all of my carefully carved crosses. I cried but I never told anyone. How could I? I had sought in my own small way to preserve the memory of what always in the end perishes: life and great deeds. I wonder what the man with the scythe did with my crosses. I wonder if they still exist."

"Yes, it was a child's effort against time," commented Auden. "And perhaps the archaeologist is just that child grown up."

It was time for Auden to go. We stood and exchanged polite amenities while he breathed in that heavy, sad way he had. "Write me at Oxford," he had said at the door. But then there was Austria and soon he was gone. Besides one does not annoy the great. Their burdens are too heavy. They listen kindly with their eyes far away.

After that dinner I was glumly despondent for days. Finally a rage possessed me, started unwittingly by that gentle, gifted man who was to die happily after a recitation of his magnificent verse. For nights I lay sleepless in a New York hotel room and all my memories in one gigantic catharsis were bad, spewed out of hell's mouth, invoked by that one dinner, that one question, *what do you remember first?* My God, they were all firsts. My brain was so scarred it was a miracle it had survived in any fashion.

For example, I remembered for the first time a ruined farmhouse that I had stumbled upon in my solitary ramblings after school. The road was one I had never taken before. Rain was falling. Leaves lay thick on the abandoned road. Hesitantly I approached and stood in the doorway. Plaster had collapsed from the ceiling; wind mourned through the empty windows. I crunched tentatively over shattered glass upon the floor. Papers lay scattered about in wild disorder. Some looked like school examination papers. I picked one up in curiosity, but this, my own mature judgment tells me, no one will believe. The name Eiseley was scrawled across the cover. I was too shocked even to read the paper. No such family had ever been mentioned by my parents. We had come from elsewhere. But here, in poverty like our own, at the edge of town, had subsisted in this ruined house a boy with my own name. Gingerly I picked up another paper. There was the scrawled name again, not too unlike my own rough signature. The date was what might have been expected in that tottering clapboard house. It read from the last decade of the century before. They were gone, whoever they were, and another Eiseley was tiptoing through the ruined house.

All that remained in a room that might in those days have been called the parlor were two dice lying forlornly amidst the plaster, forgotten at the owners' last exit. I picked up the pretty cubes uncertainly in the growing sunset through the window, and on impulse cast them. I did not know how adults played, I merely cast and cast again, making up my own game as I played. Sometimes I thought I won and murmured to myself as children will. Sometimes I thought I lost, but I liked the clicking sound before I rolled the dice. For what stakes did I play, with my childish mind gravely considering? I think I was too naive for such wishes as money and fortune. I played, and here memory almost fails me. I think I played against the universe as the universe was represented by the wind, stirring papers on the plaster-strewn floor. I played against time, remembering my stolen crosses, I played for adventure and escape. Then, clutching the dice, but not the paper with my name, I fled frantically down the leaf-sodden unused road, never to return. One of the dice survives still in my desk drawer. The time is sixty years away.

I have said that, though almost ostracized, we loved each other fiercely there in the silent midcountry because there was nothing else to love, but was it true? Was the hour of departure nearing? My mother lavished affection upon me in her tigerish silent way, giving me cakes when I should have had bread, attempting protection when I was already learning without brothers the grimness and realities of the street.

There had been the time I had just encountered the neighborhood bully. His father's shoulder had been long distorted and rheumatic from the carrying of ice, and the elder son had just encountered the law and gone to prison. My antagonist had inherited his brother's status in the black Irish gang that I had heretofore succeeded in avoiding by journeying homeward from school through alleys and occasional thickets best known to me. But now brother replaced brother. We confronted each other on someone's lawn.

"Get down on your knees," he said contemptuously, knowing very well what was coming. He had left me no way out. At that moment I hit him most inexpertly in the face, whereupon he began very scientifically, as things go in childish circles, to cut me to ribbons. My nose went first.

But then came the rage, the utter fury, summoned up from a thousand home repressions, adrenalin pumped into me from my Viking grandfather, the throwback from the long ships, the berserk men who cared nothing for living when the mood came on them and they stormed the English towns. It comes to me now that the Irishman must have seen it in my eyes. By nature I was a quiet reclusive boy, but then I went utterly mad.

The smashed nose meant nothing, the scientific lefts and rights slicing up my features meant nothing. I went through them with body punches and my eyes. When I halted we were clear across the street and the boy was gone, running for home. Typically I, too, turned homeward but not for succor. All I wanted was access to the outside watertap to wash off the blood cascading down my face. This I proceeded to do with the stoical indifference of one who expected no help.

As I went about finishing my task, my mother, peering through the curtains, saw my face, and promptly had hysterics. I turned away then. I always turned away. In the end, not too far distant, there would be an unbridgeable silence between us. Slowly I was leaving the world she knew and desperation marked her face.

I was old enough that I obeyed my father's injunction, reluctantly given out of his own pain. "Your mother is not responsible, son. Do not cross her. Do you understand?" He held me with his eyes, a man I loved, who could have taken the poor man's divorce, desertion, at any moment. The easy way out. He stayed for me. That was the simple reason. He stayed when his own closest relatives urged him to depart.

I cast down my eyes. "Yes, father," I promised, but I could not say for always. I think he knew it, but work and growing age were crushing him. We looked at each other in a blind despair.

I was like a rag doll upon whose frame skins were tightening in a distorted crippling sequence; the toddler begging for peace between his parents at midnight; the lad suppressing fury till he shook with it; the solitary with his books; the projected fugitive running desperately through the snows of 1912; the dice player in the ruined house of his own name. Who was he, really? The man, so the psychologists would say, who had to be shaped or found in five years' time. I was inarticulate but somewhere, far forward, I would meet the running man; the peace I begged for between my parents would, too often, leave me sleepless. There was another thing I could not name to Auden. The fact that I remember it at all reveals the beginning of adulthood and a sense of sin beyond my years.

To grow is a gain, an enlargement of life; is not this what they tell us? Yet it is also a departure. There is something lost that will not return. We moved one fall to Aurora, Nebraska, a sleepy country town near the Platte. A few boys gathered to watch the van unload. "Want to play?" ventured one. "Sure," I said. I followed them off over a rise to a creek bed. "We're making a cave in the bank," they explained. It was a great raw gaping hole obviously worked on by more than one generation of troglodytes. They giggled. "But first you've got to swear awful words. We'll all swear."

I was a silent boy, who went by reading. My father did not use these words. I was, in retrospect, a very funny little boy. I was so alone I did not know how to swear, but clamoring they taught me. I wanted to belong, to enter the troglodytes' existence. I shouted and mouthed the uncouth, unfamiliar words with the rest.

Mother was restless in the new environment, though again my father had wisely chosen a house at the edge of town. The population was primarily Scandinavian. She exercised arbitrary judgment. She drove good-natured, friendly boys away if they seemed big, and on the other hand encouraged slighter youngsters whom I had every reason to despise.

Finally, because it was farmland over which children roamed at will, mother's ability to keep track of my wide-ranging absences faltered. On one memorable occasion her driving, possessive restlessness passed out of bounds. She pursued us to a nearby pasture and in the rasping voice of deafness ordered me home.

My comrades of the fields stood watching. I was ten years old by then. I sensed my status in this gang was at stake. I refused to come. I had refused a parental order that was arbitrary and uncalled for and, in addition, I was humiliated. My mother was behaving in the manner of a witch. She could not hear, she was violently gesticulating without dignity, and her dress was somehow appropriate to the occasion.

Slowly I turned and looked at my companions. Their faces could not be read. They simply waited, doubtless waited for me to break the apron strings that rested lightly and tolerably upon themselves. And so in the end I broke my father's injunction; I ran, and with me ran my childish companions, over fences, tumbling down haystacks, chuckling, with the witch, her hair flying, her clothing disarrayed, stumbling after. Escape, escape, the first stirrings of the running man. Miles of escape.

Of course she gave up. Of course she never caught us. Walking home alone in the twilight I was bitterly ashamed. Ashamed for the violation of my promise to my father. Ashamed at what I had done to my savage and stone-deaf mother who could not grasp the fact that I had to make my way in a world unknown to her. Ashamed for the story that would penetrate the neighborhood. Ashamed for my own weakness. Ashamed, ashamed.

I do not remember a single teacher from that school, a single thing I learned there. Men were then drilling in a lot close to our house. I watched them every day. Finally they marched off. It was 1917. I was ten years old. I wanted to go. Either that or back to sleeping the troglodyte existence we had created in the cave bank. But never home, not ever. Even today, as though in a far-off crystal, I can see my running, gesticulating mother and her distorted features cursing us. And they laughed, you see, my companions. Perhaps I, in anxiety to belong, did also. That is what I could not tell Auden. Only an unutterable savagery, my savagery at myself, scrawls it once and once only on this page.

Loren Eiseley

The Letter

I remember," he had written. That was in 1947, and my hand shook remembering with him. Over a quarter of a century has passed and I have not answered his letter. He was the closest of all my boyhood friends. And if, in the end, I did not respond to his letter, it was not that I intended it so. I sent, in fact, a card saying I was moving to Philadelphia and would write to him later. All this was true. In a little bundle of letters kept in a box and consisting mostly of communications from men long dead, I faithfully preserved his message. Only slowly did I come to realize that something within me was too deeply wounded ever to respond. In the first place, let me state with candor that if I have let nearly thirty years drift by—I last saw Jimmy Dawes when we graduated from grade school—I was forty-one when I received his own first recognition of my existence. He had seen some pieces of mine in a national magazine, *Harper's,* and remembered my name. Perhaps in a sense this balances the equation.

He wrote me as a successful officer in a huge corporate enterprise. He remembered a surprising amount about our childhood activities and he recalled something that touched my naturalist's memories and sent me groping to my book shelf. "I remember," he wrote, "all those squirmy things we collected in jars and buckets and took home to put in the aquariums you made."

He was right even if he was chuckling a little. But he was not content

with these boyish memories. He persisted until he came to the explanation, unexpected by me, as to why, though we had lived on into
young adulthood in the same community, I had never encountered
him after our eighth-grade graduation.

I have said earlier that though in the western towns of those years
poor children might attend school with those of another economic
level, there came a time when the bridge was automatically withdrawn. This I accepted and never questioned though much later when
I passed my companion's home I used to look up at it a little wistfully.
I had once been welcome there —I suppose, looking back, like a dog,
a pet good for one's son at a certain stage of life, but not to be confused
with the major business of growing up. No, I should not put it so
harshly; his mother, his sisters were kind. I know that in their home I
saw my first *Atlantic Monthly* in the traditional red-brick covers.

I rarely saw Jimmy Dawes' father, but I knew him as a contained, se-
rious man of business. He ruled a healthy, well-directed household in
which one knew that because of the wisdom of father everyone would
marry well, be economically secure, and that each child was bound to
live happily ever after. Actually, because of the peculiarities of my
edge-of-town status, these good people had probably stretched things
a little to please their only son, since we played happily together. If I
led him to adventures in the fields and ponds around the town, these
were no more than an *Atlantic* essayist of the time would have thoroughly approved.

When Jimmy vanished from my ken I suppose I ached a little, but I
was adjusted to the inevitable loneliness of my circumstances. There
was a very large high school in Lincoln and I never saw him again.
Looking back, it is possible he was sent elsewhere. I repeat that the separation was so neatly handled that I never thought of it as more than
the usual process of growing up, of being always the aloof observer,
never participant in the success of other families. No, if Jimmy Dawes
had written me after all those years merely to wish me well and re-

member our pond adventures, I would have answered. Not effusively—one comes to accept one's place in life—but to congratulate him upon his success, the fine children of whom he wrote, and to thank him for his interest in my few ephemeral essays. There the matter would have ended. I know he meant well, but having grown up in that ordered household he proceeded, either in tactless condescension or, more likely, by way of explaining a thirty-year silence, to examine his father's role in the matter.

The social facts of life had left me merely grateful for a few shared years and timid, occasional entrances into a home fantastically different from my own. I had realized, even as a youngster, that Jimmy Dawes was headed for something I would never be. But now here was Jimmy Dawes, after thirty years, telling me with no trace of regret that he had only pursued his father's directive. Father had deemed it time that his son discontinue this enthusiasm for a pond-dipping fox-child and get on with the business of where a properly directed young man should go.

Papa had said it, apparently, right out loud. Oh, it is true that at the end of the letter Jimmy Dawes had suggested, in a belated attempt to mollify my feelings, that perhaps he had himself been responsible in having taken up with all these matters too enthusiastically. Doubtless father had been right. Fathers, in his world, always were. He managed to tell me that also.

At the end of the letter I found myself shaken over what to Jimmy was a simple fact that I would easily appreciate. Could I now venture pretentiously to Jimmy Dawes, that I was, after all, a social scientist? Could I say that I had long since accepted all that he had to tell me, and then ask him upon what impulse he had chosen to repeat what his father had said? And if you chose to forget your friend, the nagging thought persisted, why are you busy with this resurrection now? Am I made respectable at last by my printed name, because the *Atlantic Monthly* was taken and read in your father's house long ago?

I had liked Jimmy Dawes; that was why his belated emergence was so painful. There was still in that letter some trace of a bounding, youthful eagerness long lost by me. I sent the brief card of acknowledgment, went on my way to Penn, and proceeded to be haunted the rest of my life by his letter. No, not quite. In preparation for eventual retirement I began in the late summer of 1974 to destroy old files. I knew where the letter was, though I had not read it again in all those years. I read it once more, and because Jimmy had been my boyhood chum I reached for the telephone and asked for a number and an address far away. "Sir," the operator's voice came back, "no such name exists at that address."

At heart I knew it would be so, but at least I had finally nerved myself to try. His children would be grown and married. He would be retired and playing golf in Florida, or perhaps reading a vastly changed *Atlantic Monthly,* like his father, in an equally traditional, well-managed home. Slowly, deliberately, I tore up the long-cherished letter. It had served its purpose. Through it I began to remember where part of my interest in the living world began.

On the shelf where I had started to fumble when Jimmy Dawes' letter arrived was an old book, bound in green cloth with a stylized fish in gold stamped on the cover, a book bearing the unimpressive title *The Home Aquarium: How to Care for It.* A man equally obscure had published that book in 1902, five years before I was born. His name was Eugene Smith and whatever else he did in life I do not know. The introduction was written in Hoboken, New Jersey.

The copy I possess is not the one I borrowed and read from the Lincoln City Library while I was still in grade school. So profound had been its influence upon me, however, that in adulthood, after coming East, I had sought for it unsuccessfully in old book stores. One day, in my first year in graduate school, I had been turning over books on a sales' table largely strewn with trivia in Leary's famous old store in Philadelphia, a store now vanished. To my utter surprise there lay three copies with the stamp of the golden fish upon their covers. It was all I could do to restrain myself from purchasing all three. It was the first and last time I ever saw the work in a book store. The name B. W. Griffiths and the date 1903 was inscribed on the fly leaf. To this I added my own scrawled signature and the date 1933. Now, in the year 1975, I still possess it. I have spoken in the past of hidden teachers. This book was one such to me.

It is true there had been my early delvings in sandpiles, and so strong is childhood memory, that I can still recollect the precise circumstances under which I first discovered a trapdoor spider's nest. My amazing, unpredictable mother was the person who explained it to me. How, then, did this pedestrian work on the home aquarium happen to light up my whole inner existence?

There were, I think, two very precise reasons having nothing to do with literature as such that intrigued me about this old volume. Most of the aquarium books of today start with the assumption that you go to a pet store and buy tanks, thermometers, specialized aeration equipment, and even your assemblage of flora and fauna "ready made." Smith's book contained no such assumption. You got the glass, you cut it yourself, you made bottoms and sides of wood. Then, somewhere, you obtained tar to waterproof the wood and the joints. Moreover, Smith had given a simple running account, not alone of easily accessible fresh-water fish, but of local invertebrates with which aquariums could be stocked.

I genuinely believe that it was from the pages of his book that I first learned about the green fresh water polyp *Hydra viridis,* so that later I identified it in one of my own aquariums, not from the wild. In other words, there had been placed within my hands the possibility of being the director, the overseer of living worlds of my own. If one has the temperament and takes this seriously one will feel forever afterward responsible for the life that cannot survive without one's constant attention. One learns unconsciously about ecological balance, what things may the most readily survive together, and, if one spends long hours observing, as I later came to do, one makes one's own discoveries and is not confined to textbooks.

This leads me to the other value gained from Smith's plain little volume. I spent no time, as a midlander, yearning after tropical marine fish or other exotic specimens. I would have to make my own aquariums and stock them as well. Furthermore, for a lad inclined as I was, one need not confine oneself to fish. One could also make smaller aquariums devoted to invertebrate pond life.

By chance I encountered Smith's book in midwinter and it would be a normal parental expectation that all of this interest in "slippery things" would have worn itself out while the natural world was asleep under pond ice. In the flaming heat of enthusiasm, however, I grew determined not to wait upon nature. I first secured some wood and glass scraps from a nearby building project and tar from a broken tar barrel. Though I had no great gifts as a carpenter I did the job by persistence from materials then strewn casually about every house under construction. I boiled and applied the warm tar myself. In one triumph, I even made a small aquarium from a cigar box.

In a few days I had enough worlds to start any number of creations. To do so I had to reverse the course of nature. Elders may quail but this is nothing for children. So it was winter? Snow lying thick over the countryside? Ponds under ice? Never mind. I knew where the streams and ponds were. I had also learned that many forms of life hibernate in the mud of ponds. All that was necessary was to improvise a net, again homemade, take a small lard bucket or two, and trudge off to the most accessible Walden.

The countryside was open in those days. On one visit to Lincoln several years ago I thought it might be good to tramp out to that old pond where so many generations of boys had swam, waded, or collected. Forbidding fences warned me away. It was now part of a country club of the sort doubtless frequented by the successors of the parents of

Jimmy Dawes. I speak no ill. If a country club had not acquired the ponds and landscaped the greens, all would have been filled in by suburban developments in any case. But this was all wild once, and the feeling that is left is somehow lost and bittersweet. The pond is there. It is not the same pond. It is "reserved." It has been tamed for rich men to play beside. Either that or the developers come. One takes one's choice. No. Not really. One has no choice.

On that winter day so long ago I almost lost my life. I arrived at the pond and chopped an experimental hole near the shore where I worked my clumsy mud-dredging apparatus back and forth. My plan was successful. I was drawing up a few sleeping water boatmen, whirligig beetles, and dragonfly larvae, along with other more microscopic animalcules. These I placed in my lard buckets and prepared to go home and begin the stocking of my little aquariums. A forced spring had come early to my captives.

There were skates on a strap hanging around my neck, and before leaving I thought I would take one quick run over the pond. It was a very cold day, the ice firm. I had no reason to anticipate disaster. I made two swift passages out over what I knew to be deeper water. On the second pass, as I stepped up speed, there was a sudden, instantaneous splintering of ice. The leg to which I had just applied skating pressure went hip deep into the water. I came down upon my face. I lay there a moment half stunned. No one was with me. What if the rest of the ice broke? Even if one held on to the edge one would freeze very quickly.

I waited anxiously, trying not to extend the ice-fracture by struggling. I was scared enough to yell, but it was useless. No one but a boy infused with the momentary idea of becoming a creator would be out on a day like this. Slowly I slid forward arms spread, and withdrew my soaking leg from the hole. I must have struck an ice bubble with that one foot. The freezing weather fortunately permitted no general collapse of the ice. In one sweating moment I was safe, but I had to jog all the way home with my closed buckets.

After such an event there was no one's arms in which to fall at home. If one did, there would be only hysterical admonitions, and I would be lucky to be allowed out. Slowly my inner life was continuing to adjust to this fact. I had to rely on silence. It was like creeping away from death out of an ice hole an inch at a time. You did it alone.

Critics, good friends in academia, sometimes ask, as is so frequently the custom, what impelled me to become a writer, what I read, who influenced me. Again, if pressed, I feel as though I were still inching out of that smashed ice bubble. Any educated man is bound to live in the cultural stream of his time. If I say, however, that I have read Thoreau, then it has been Thoreau who has been my mentor; this in spite of the fact that I did not read Thoreau until well into my middle years. Or it is Melville, Poe, anyone but me. If I mention a living writer whom I know, he is my inspiration, my fount of knowledge.

Or it is the editor of my first book who must have taught me this arcane art, because if one writes one must indeed publish a first book and that requires an editor. Or if one remains perplexed and has no answer, then one is stupid and one's work is written by a ghost who is paid well for his silence. In one institution where I taught long ago, it was generally assumed that all of us young science instructors were too manly to engage in this dubious art. Our wives produced our papers.

I myself believe implicitly in what G. K. Chesterton wrote many years ago: "The man who makes a vow makes an appointment with himself at some distant time or place." I think this vow of which Chesterton speaks was made unconsciously by me three separate times in my childhood. These unconscious vows may not have determined the precise mode of whatever achievement may be accorded mine, or what crossroads I may have encountered on the way. I mean to imply simply that when a vow is made one will someday meet what it has made of oneself and, most likely, curse one's failure. In any event, one will meet one's self. Let me tell about the first of those vows. It was a vow to read, and surely the first step to writing is a vow to read, not to encounter an editor.

It so happened that when I was five years old my parents, in a rare moment of doting agreement, looked upon their solitary child and decided not to pack him off to kindergarten in that year. One can call them feckless, kind, or wise, according to one's notions of the result. Surprisingly, I can remember the gist of their conversation because I caught in its implications the feel of that looming weather which, in after years, we know as life.

"Let him be free another year," they said. I remember my astonishment at their agreement. "There'll be all his life to learn about the rest. Let him be free to play just one more time." They both smiled in sudden affection. The words come back from very far away. I rather think they are my mother's, though there is a soft inflection in them. For once, just once, there was total unanimity between my parents. A rare thing. And I pretended not to have heard that phrase "about the rest." Nevertheless when I went out to play in the sunshine I felt chilled.

I did not have to go to kindergarten to learn to read. I had already mastered the alphabet at some earlier point. I had little primers of my own, the see-John-run sort of thing or its equivalent in that year of 1912. Yes, in that fashion I could read. Sometime in the months that followed, my elder brother paid a brief visit home. He brought with him a full adult version of *Robinson Crusoe*. He proceeded to read it to me in spare moments. I lived for that story. I hung upon my brother's words. Then abruptly, as was always happening in the world above me in the lamplight, my brother had departed. We had reached only as far as the discovery of the footprint on the shore.

He left me the book, to be exact, but no reader. I never asked mother to read because her voice distressed me. Her inability to hear had made it harsh and jangling. My father read with great grace and beauty but he worked the long and dreadful hours of those years. There was only one thing evident to me. I had to get on with it, do it myself, otherwise I would never learn what happened to Crusoe.

I took Defoe's book and some little inadequate dictionary I found about the house, and proceeded to worry and chew my way like a puppy through the remaining pages. No doubt I lost the sense of a word here and there, but I mastered it. I had read it on my own. Papa bought me *Twenty Thousand Leagues Under the Sea* as a reward. I read that, too. I began to read everything I could lay my hands on.

Well, that was a kind of vow made to myself, was it not? Not just to handle ABC's, not to do the minimum for a school teacher, but to read books, read them for the joy of reading. When critics come to me again I shall say, "Put Daniel Defoe on the list, and myself, as well," because I kept the vow to read *Robinson Crusoe* and then to try to read all the books in the local library, or at least to examine them. I even learned to scan the papers for what a boy might hopefully understand.

That was 1912 and in the arctic winter of that year three prisoners blasted their way through the gates of the state penitentiary in our town. They left the warden and his deputy dead behind them. A blizzard howled across the landscape. This was long before the time of the fast getaway by car. The convicts were out somewhere shivering in the driving snow with the inevitable ruthless hunters drawing a narrowing circle for the kill.

That night papa tossed the paper on the table with a sigh. "They won't make it," he said and I could see by his eyes he was out there in the snow.

"But papa," I said, "the papers say they are bad men. They killed the warden."

"Yes, son," he said heavily. Then he paused, censoring his words carefully. "There are also bad prisons and bad wardens. You read your books now. Sit here by the lamp. Stay warm. Someday you will know more about people out in the cold. Try to think kindly, until then.

These papers," he tapped the one he had brought in, "will not tell you everything. Someday when you are grown up you may remember this."

"Yes, papa," I said, and that was the second vow, though again I did not know it. The memory of that night stayed on, as did the darkness and the howling wind. Long after those fleeing men were dead I would re-enter that year to seek them out. I would dream once more about them. I would be—Never mind, I would be myself a fugitive. When once, just once, through sympathy, one enters the cold, one is always there. One eternally keeps an appointment with one's self, but I was much too young to know.

By the time of the aquarium episode I was several years older. That, too, was a vow, the sudden furious vow that induced me to create spring in midwinter. Record the homely writing of Eugene Smith, placing in my hand a tool and giving me command of tiny kingdoms. When I finally went away to graduate school I left them to the care of my grandmother Corey. I told her just how to manage them. She did so faithfully until her death. I think they brightened her final years— the little worlds we cared for. After the breakup of the house I searched for them. No one could tell me where they were. I would have greatly treasured them in the years remaining. I have never had an aquarium since, though expensive ones are now to be had.

I suppose, if I wrote till midnight and beyond, I could conjure up one last unstable vow—when at nineteen I watched, outwardly un-moved, the letter of my father crumble in the flames. I started, did I not, to explain why a man writes and how there is always supposed to be someone he had derived his inspiration from, following which the good scholar may seek out the predecessor of one's predecessor, until nothing original is left. I have said we all live in a moving stream, as surely as a catfish groping with its whiskers in the muddy dark. I have seized this opportunity nevertheless to ensure that my unhappy par-ents' part in this dubious creation of a writer is not forgotten, nor the role of my half-brother, who accidentally stimulated me into a gigantic reading effort. As for Eugene Smith, he gave me the gift of wanting to understand other lives, even if he almost stole my own upon that winter pond.

I would like to tell this dead man that I fondled his little handbook as I wrote this chapter. We are not important names, I would like to tell him. His is a very common one and all we are quickly vanishes. But still not quite. That is the wonder of words. They drift on and on beyond imagining. Did Eugene Smith of Hoboken think his book would have a lifelong impact on a boy in a small Nebraska town? I do not think so.

Ironically, one of the senior officers of the firm that published Smith's work asked me not long ago if he could interest me in a project and would I come to lunch. The letter was pleasantly flattering. I wrote the man that I would be glad to lunch with him, though in all honesty I was heavily committed elsewhere. After his original invitation, I was never accorded the dignity of a reply.

Sometimes this is called the world of publishing. It is a pity. I would have liked to tell this important man, over a cocktail, about a man named Smith whose book was published by his very own house before he, this generation's president, had been born. I would have been delighted to inform him that there was a stylized gold fish on the cover, and to what place the book had traveled, and how it had almost drowned, as well as uplifted, a small boy. Alas, this is a foolish dream. The presidents of great companies do not go to luncheons for such purposes. As for me, these strange chances in life intrigue me. I delight or shudder to hear of them.

I am sorry also, Jimmy Dawes, that your letter went unanswered. I genuinely hope that you and your grown-up family are happy. I apologize for the mind-block that descended upon me there in Ohio, that old psychic wound that should have been overlooked had I been stronger. But at the last I tried. Perhaps that is what my parents meant when they said, "There'll be all his life to learn about the rest." I learned part when my father died, the part about the cold. Jimmy Dawes was still in my home town, a few blocks from where I lived, but no note of condolence ever came from him or his family. I kept your letter, Jimmy. Almost thirty years later I tried to call you long distance. And now at last the wound is closing. It is very late.

Reflections of a Wanderer

The Star Thrower

Who is the man walking in the Way?
An eye glaring in the skull.

SECCHO

It has ever been my lot, though formally myself a teacher, to be taught surely by none. There are times when I have thought to read lessons in the sky, or in books, or from the behavior of my fellows, but in the end my perceptions have frequently been inadequate or betrayed. Nevertheless, I venture to say that of what man may be I have caught a fugitive glimpse, not among multitudes of men, but along an endless wave-beaten coast at dawn. As always, there is this apparent break, this rift in nature, before the insight comes. The terrible question has to translate itself into an even more terrifying freedom.

If there is any meaning to this book [*The Unexpected Universe*], it began on the beaches of Costabel with just such a leap across an unknown abyss. It began, if I may borrow the expression from a Buddhist sage, with the skull and the eye. I was the skull. I was the inhumanly stripped skeleton without voice, without hope, wandering alone upon the shores of the world. I was devoid of pity, because pity implies hope. There was, in this desiccated skull, only an eye like a pharos light, a beacon, a search beam revolving endlessly in sunless noonday or black night. Ideas like swarms of insects rose to the beam, but the light consumed them. Upon that shore meaning had ceased. There were only the dead skull and the revolving eye. With such an eye, some have said, science looks upon the world. I do not know. I know only that I was the skull of emptiness and the endlessly revolving light without pity.

Once, in a dingy restaurant in the town, I had heard a woman say: "My father reads a goose bone for the weather." A modern primitive, I had thought, a diviner, using a method older than Stonehenge, as old as the arctic forests.

"And where does he do that?" the woman's companion had asked amusedly.

"In Costabel," she answered complacently, "in Costabel." The voice came back and buzzed faintly for a moment in the dark under the revolving eye. It did not make sense, but nothing in Costabel made sense. Perhaps that was why I had finally found myself in Costabel. Perhaps all men are destined at some time to arrive there as I did.

I had come by quite ordinary means, but I was still the skull with the eye. I concealed myself beneath a fisherman's cap and sunglasses, so that I looked like everyone else on the beach. This is the way things are managed in Costabel. It is on the shore that the revolving eye begins its beam and the whispers rise in the empty darkness of the skull.

The beaches of Costabel are littered with the debris of life. Shells are cast up in windrows; a hermit crab, fumbling for a new home in the depths, is tossed naked ashore, where the waiting gulls cut him to pieces. Along the strip of wet sand that marks the ebbing and flowing of the tide, death walks hugely and in many forms. Even the torn fragments of green sponge yield bits of scrambling life striving to return to the great mother that has nourished and protected them.

In the end the sea rejects its offspring. They cannot fight their way home through the surf which casts them repeatedly back upon the shore. The tiny breathing pores of starfish are stuffed with sand. The rising sun shrivels the mucilaginous bodies of the unprotected. The sea beach and its endless war are soundless. Nothing screams but the gulls.

In the night, particularly in the tourist season, or during great storms, one can observe another vulturine activity. One can see, in the hour before dawn on the ebb tide, electric torches bobbing like fireflies along the beach. It is the sign of the professional shellers seeking to outrun and anticipate their less aggressive neighbors. A kind of greedy madness sweeps over the competing collectors. After a storm one can see them hurrying along with bundles of gathered starfish, or, toppling and overburdened, clutching bags of living shells whose hidden occupants will be slowly cooked and dissolved in the outdoor kettles provided by the resort hotels for the cleaning of specimens. Following one such episode I met the star thrower.

As soon as the ebb was flowing, as soon as I could make out in my sleeplessness the flashlights on the beach, I arose and dressed in the dark. As I came down the steps to the shore I could hear the deeper rumble of the surf. A gaping hole filled with churning sand had cut sharply into the breakwater. Flying sand as light as powder coated every exposed object like snow. I made my way around the altered edges of the cove and proceeded on my morning walk up the shore. Now and then a stooping figure moved in the gloom or a rain squall swept past me with light pattering steps. There was a faint sense of coming light somewhere behind me in the east.

Soon I began to make out objects, upended timbers, conch shells, sea wrack wrenched from the far-out kelp forests. A pink-clawed crab encased in a green cup of sponge lay sprawling where the waves had tossed him. Long-limbed starfish were strewn everywhere, as though the night sky had showered down. I paused once briefly. A small octopus, its beautiful dark-lensed eyes bleared with sand, gazed up at me from a ragged bundle of tentacles. I hesitated, and touched it briefly with my foot. It was dead. I paced on once more before the spreading whitecaps of the surf.

The shore grew steeper, the sound of the sea heavier and more menacing, as I rounded a bluff into the full blast of the offshore wind. I was away from the shellers now and strode more rapidly over the wet sand that effaced my footprints. Around the next point there might be a refuge from the wind. The sun behind me was pressing upward at the horizon's rim—an ominous red glare amidst the tumbling blackness of the clouds. Ahead of me, over the projecting point, a gigantic rainbow of incredible perfection had sprung shimmering into existence. Somewhere toward its foot I discerned a human figure standing, as it seemed to me, within the rainbow, though unconscious of his position. He was gazing fixedly at something in the sand.

Eventually he stooped and flung the object beyond the breaking surf. I labored toward him over a half mile of uncertain footing. By the time I reached him the rainbow had receded ahead of us, but something of its color still ran hastily in many changing lights across his features. He was starting to kneel again.

In a pool of sand and silt a starfish had thrust its arms up stiffly and was holding its body away from the stifling mud.

"It's still alive," I ventured.

"Yes," he said, and with a quick yet gentle movement he picked up the star and spun it over my head and far out into the sea. It sank in a burst of spume, and the waters roared once more.

"It may live," he said, "if the offshore pull is strong enough." He spoke gently, and across his bronzed worn face the light still came and went in subtly altering colors.

"There are not many come this far," I said, groping in a sudden embarrassment for words. "Do you collect?"

"Only like this," he said softly, gesturing amidst the wreckage of the shore. "And only for the living." He stooped again, oblivious of my curiosity, and skipped another star neatly across the water.

"The stars," he said, "throw well. One can help them."

He looked full at me with a faint question kindling in his eyes, which seemed to take on the far depths of the sea.

"I do not collect," I said uncomfortably, the wind beating at my garments. "Neither the living nor the dead. I gave it up a long time ago. Death is the only successful collector." I could feel the full night blackness in my skull and the terrible eye resuming its indifferent journey. I nodded and walked away, leaving him there upon the dune with that great rainbow ranging up the sky behind him.

I turned as I neared a bend in the coast and saw him toss another star, skimming it skillfully far out over the ravening and tumultuous water. For a moment, in the changing light, the sower appeared magnified, as though casting larger stars upon some greater sea. He had, at any rate, the posture of a god.

But again the eye, the cold world-shriveling eye, began its inevitable circling in my skull. He is a man, I considered sharply, bringing my thought to rest. The star thrower is a man, and death is running more fleet than he along every seabeach in the world.

I adjusted the dark lens of my glasses and, thus disguised, I paced slowly back by the starfish gatherers, past the shell collectors, with their vulgar little spades and the stick-length shelling pincers that eased their elderly backs while they snatched at treasures in the sand. I chose to look full at the steaming kettles in which beautiful voiceless things were being boiled alive. Behind my sunglasses a kind of litany began and refused to die down. "*As I came through the desert thus it was, as I came through the desert.*"

In the darkness of my room I lay quiet with the sunglasses removed, but the eye turned and turned. In the desert, an old monk had once advised a traveler, the voices of God and the Devil are scarcely distinguishable. Costabel was a desert. I lay quiet, but my restless hand at the bedside fingered the edge of an invisible abyss. "Certain coasts," the remark of a perceptive writer came back to me, "are set apart for shipwreck." With unerring persistence I had made my way thither.

II

There is a difference in our human outlook, depending on whether we have been born upon level plains, where one step reasonably leads to another, or whether, by contrast, we have spent our lives amidst glacial crevasses and precipitous descents. In the case of the mountaineer, one step does not always lead rationally to another save by a desperate leap over a chasm or by an even more hesitant tiptoeing across precarious snow bridges.

Something about these opposed landscapes has its analogue in the mind of man. Our prehistoric life, one might say, began amidst enforested gloom with the abandonment of the protected instinctive life of nature. We sought, instead, an adventurous existence amidst the crater lands and ice fields of self-generated ideas. Clambering onward, we have slowly made our way out of a maze of isolated peaks into the level plains of science. Here, one step seems definitely to succeed another, the universe appears to take on an imposed order, and the illusions through which mankind has painfully made its way for many centuries have given place to the enormous vistas of past and future time. The encrusted eye in the stone speaks to us of undeviating sunlight; the calculated elliptic of Halley's comet no longer forecasts world disaster. The planet plunges on through a chill void of star years, and there is little or nothing that remains unmeasured.

Nothing, that is, but the mind of man. Since boyhood I had been traveling across the endless coordinated realms of science, just as, in the body, I was a plains dweller, accustomed to plodding through distances unbroken by precipices. Now that I come to look back, there was one contingent aspect of that landscape I inhabited whose significance, at the time, escaped me. "Twisters," we called them locally. They were a species of cyclonic, bouncing air funnel that could suddenly loom out of nowhere, crumpling windmills or slashing with devastating fury through country towns. Sometimes, by modest contrast, more harmless varieties known as dust devils might pursue one in a gentle spinning dance for miles. One could see them hesitantly stalking across the alkali flats on a hot day, debating, perhaps, in their tall, rotating columns, whether to ascend and assume more formidable shapes. They were the trickster part of an otherwise pedestrian landscape.

Infrequent though the visitations of these malign creations of the air might be, all prudent homesteaders in those parts had provided themselves with cyclone cellars. In the careless neighborhood in which I grew up, however, we contented ourselves with the queer yarns of cyclonic folklore and the vagaries of weather prophecy. As a boy, aroused by these tales and cherishing a subterranean fondness for caves, I once attempted to dig a storm cellar. Like most such projects this one was never completed. The trickster element in nature, I realize now, had so buffeted my parents that they stoically rejected planning. Unconsciously, they had arrived at the philosophy that foresight merely invited the attention of some baleful intelligence that despised and persecuted the calculating planner. It was not until many years later that I came to realize that a kind of maleficent primordial power persists in the mind as well as in the wandering dust storms of the exterior world.

A hidden dualism that has haunted man since antiquity runs across his religious conceptions as the conflict between good and evil. It persists in the modern world of science under other guises. It becomes chaos versus form or antichaos. Form, since the rise of the evolutionary philosophy, has itself taken on an illusory quality. Our apparent shapes no longer have the stability of a single divine fiat. Instead, they waver and dissolve into the unexpected. We gaze backward into a contracting cone of life until words leave us and all we know is dissolved into the simple circuits of a reptilian brain. Finally, sentience subsides into animalcule.

Or we revolt and refuse to look deeper, but the void remains. We are rag dolls made out of many ages and skins, changelings who have slept in wood nests or hissed in the uncouth guise of waddling amphibians. We have played such roles for infinitely longer ages than we have been men. Our identity is a dream. We are process, not reality, for reality is an illusion of the daylight—the light of our particular day. In a fortnight, as aeons are measured, we may lie silent in a bed of stone, or, as has happened in the past, be figured in another guise. Two forces struggle perpetually in our bodies: Yam, the old sea dragon of the original Biblical darkness, and, arrayed against him, some wisp of dancing light that would have us linger, wistful, in our human form. "Tarry thou, till I come again"—an old legend survives among us of the admonition given by Jesus to the Wandering Jew. The words are applicable to all of us. Deep-hidden in the human psyche there is a similar injunction no longer having to do with the longevity of the body but, rather, a plea to wait upon some transcendent lesson preparing in the mind itself.

Yet the facts we face seem terrifyingly arrayed against us. It is as if at our backs, masked and demonic, moved the trickster as I have seen his role performed among the remnant of a savage people long ago. It was that of the jokester present at the most devout of ceremonies. This creature never laughed; he never made a sound. Painted in black, he followed silently behind the officiating priest, mimicking, with the added flourish of a little whip, the gestures of the devout one. His timed and stylized posturings conveyed a derision infinitely more formidable than actual laughter.

In modern terms, the dance of contingency, of the indeterminable, outwits us all. The approaching, fateful whirlwind on the plain had mercifully passed me by in youth. In the moment when I had witnessed that fireside performance I knew with surety that primitive man had lived with a dark message. He had acquiesced in the admission into his village of a cosmic messenger. Perhaps the primitives were wiser in the ways of the trickster universe than ourselves; perhaps they knew, as we do not, how to ground or make endurable the lightning.

At all events, I had learned, as I watched that half understood drama by the leaping fire, why man, even modern man, reads goose bones for the weather of his soul. Afterward I had gone out, a troubled unbeliever, into the night. There was a shadow I could not henceforth shake off, which I knew was posturing and would always posture behind me. That mocking shadow looms over me as I write. It scrawls with a derisive pen and an exaggerated flourish. I know instinctively it will be present to caricature the solemnities of my deathbed. In a quarter of a century it has never spoken.

Black magic, the magic of the primeval chaos, blots out or transmogrifies the true form of things. At the stroke of twelve the princess must flee the banquet or risk discovery in the rags of a kitchen wench; coach reverts to pumpkin. Instability lies at the heart of the world. With uncanny foresight folklore has long toyed symbolically with what the nineteenth century was to proclaim a reality, namely, that form is an illusion of the time dimension, that the magic flight of the pursued hero or heroine through frogskin and wolf coat has been, and will continue to be, the flight of all men.

Goethe's genius sensed, well before the publication of the *Origin of Species,* the thesis and antithesis that epitomize the eternal struggle of the immediate species against its dissolution into something other: in modern terms, fish into reptile, ape into man. The power to change is both creative and destructive—a sinister gift, which, unrestricted, leads onward toward the formless and inchoate void of the possible. This force can only be counterbalanced by an equal impulse toward specificity. Form, once arisen, clings to its identity. Each species and each individual holds tenaciously to its present nature. Each strives to contain the creative and abolishing maelstrom that pours unseen through the generations. The past vanishes; the present momentarily persists; the future is potential only. In this specious present of the real, life struggles to maintain every manifestation, every individuality, that exists. In the end, life always fails, but the amorphous hurrying stream is held and diverted into new organic vessels in which form persists, though the form may not be that of yesterday.

The evolutionists, piercing beneath the show of momentary stability, discovered, hidden in rudimentary organs, the discarded rubbish of the past. They detected the reptile under the lifted feathers of the bird, the lost terrestrial limbs dwindling beneath the blubber of the giant cetaceans. They saw life rushing outward from an unknown center, just as today the astronomer senses the galaxies fleeing into the infinity of darkness. As the spinning galactic clouds hurl stars and worlds across the night, so life, equally impelled by the centrifugal powers lurking in the germ cell, scatters the splintered radiance of consciousness and sends it prowling and contending through the thickets of the world.

All this devious, tattered way was exposed to the ceaselessly turning eye within the skull that lay hidden upon the bed in Costabel. Slowly that eye grew conscious of another eye that searched it with equal penetration from the shadows of the room. It may have been a projection from the mind within the skull, but the eye was, nevertheless, exteriorized and haunting. It began as something glaucous and blind beneath a web of clinging algae. It altered suddenly and became the sand-smeared eye of the dead cephalopod I had encountered upon the beach. The transformations became more rapid with the concentration of my attention, and they became more formidable. There was the beaten, bloodshot eye of an animal from somewhere within my childhood experience. Finally, there was an eye that seemed torn from a photograph, but that looked through me as though it had already raced in vision up to the steep edge of nothingness and absorbed whatever terror lay in that abyss. I sank back again upon my cot and buried my head in the pillow. I knew the eye and the circumstance and the question. It was my mother. She was long dead, and the way backward was lost.

III

Now it may be asked, upon the coasts that invite shipwreck, why the ships should come, just as we may ask the man who pursues knowledge why he should be left with a revolving search beam in the head whose light falls only upon disaster or the flotsam of the shore. There is an answer, but its way is not across the level plains of science, for the science of remote abysses no longer shelters man. Instead, it reveals him in vaporous metamorphic succession as the homeless and unspecified one, the creature of the magic flight.

Long ago, when the future was just a simple tomorrow, men had cast intricately carved game counters to determine its course, or they had traced with a grimy finger the cracks on the burnt shoulder blade of a hare. It was a prophecy of tomorrow's hunt, just as was the old farmer's anachronistic reading of the weather from the signs on the breastbone of a goose. Such quaint almanacs of nature's intent had sufficed mankind since antiquity. They would do so no longer, nor would formal apologies to the souls of the game men hunted. The hunters had come, at last, beyond the satisfying supernatural world that had always surrounded the little village, into a place of homeless frontiers and precipitous edges, the indescribable world of the natural. Here tools increasingly revenged themselves upon their creators and tomorrow became unmanageable. Man had come in his journeying to a region of terrible freedoms.

It was a place of no traditional shelter, save those erected with the aid of tools, which had also begun to achieve a revolutionary independence from their masters. Their ways had grown secretive and incalculable. Science, more powerful than the magical questions that might be addressed by a shaman to a burnt shoulder blade, could create these tools but had not succeeded in controlling their ambivalent nature. Moreover, they responded all too readily to that urge for tampering and dissolution which is part of our primate heritage.

We had been safe in the enchanted forest only because of our weakness. When the powers of that gloomy region were given to us, immediately, as in a witch's house, things began to fly about unbidden. The tools, if not science itself, were linked intangibly to the subconscious poltergeist aspect of man's nature. The closer man and the natural world drew together, the more erratic became the behavior of each. Huge shadows leaped triumphantly after every blinding illumination. It was a magnified but clearly recognizable version of the black trickster's antics behind the solemn backs of the priesthood. Here, there was one difference. The shadows had passed out of all human semblance; no societal ritual safely contained their posturings, as in the warning dance of the trickster. Instead, unseen by many because it was so gigantically real, the multiplied darkness threatened to submerge the carriers of the light.

Darwin, Einstein, and Freud might be said to have released the shadows. Yet man had already entered the perilous domain that henceforth would contain his destiny. Four hundred years ago Francis Bacon had already anticipated its dual nature. The individuals do not matter. If they had not made their discoveries, others would have surely done so. They were good men, and they came as enlighteners of mankind. The tragedy was only that at their backs the ritual figure with the whip was invisible. There was no longer anything to subdue the pride of man. The world had been laid under the heavy spell of the natural; henceforth, it would be ordered by man.

Humanity was suddenly entranced by light and fancied it reflected light. Progress was its watchword, and for a time the shadows seemed to recede. Only a few guessed that the retreat of darkness presaged the emergence of an entirely new and less tangible terror. Things, in the words of G. K. Chesterton, were to grow incalculable by being calculated. Man's powers were finite; the forces he had released in nature recognized no such limitations. They were the irrevocable monsters conjured up by a completely amateur sorcerer.

But what, we may ask, was the nature of the first discoveries that now threaten to induce disaster? Preeminent among them was, of course, the perception to which we have already referred: the discovery of the interlinked and evolving web of life. The great Victorian biologists saw, and yet refused to see, the war between form and formlessness, chaos and antichaos, which the poet Goethe had sensed contesting beneath the smiling surface of nature. "The dangerous gift from above," he had termed it, with uneasy foresight.

By contrast, Darwin, the prime student of the struggle for existence, sought to visualize in a tangled bank of leaves the silent and insatiable war of nature. Still, he could imply with a veiled complacency that man might "with some confidence" look forward to a secure future "of inappreciable length." This he could do upon the same page in the *Origin of Species* where he observes that "of the species now living very few will transmit progeny to a far distant futurity." The contradiction escaped him; he did not wish to see it. Darwin, in addition, saw life as a purely selfish struggle, in which nothing is modified for the good of another species without being directly advantageous to its associated form.

If, he contended, one part of any single species had been formed for the exclusive good of another, "it would annihilate my theory." Powerfully documented and enhanced though the statement has become, famine, war, and death are not the sole instruments biologists today would accept as the means toward that perfection of which Darwin spoke. The subject is subtle and intricate, however, and one facet of it must be reserved for another chapter. Let it suffice to say here that the sign of the dark cave and the club became so firmly fixed in human thinking that in our time it has been invoked as signifying man's true image in books selling in the hundreds of thousands.

From the thesis and antithesis contained in Darwinism we come to Freud. The public knows that, like Darwin, the master of the inner world took the secure, stable, and sunlit province of the mind and revealed it as a place of contending furies. Ghostly transformations, flitting night shadows, misshapen changelings existed there, as real as anything that haunted the natural universe of Darwin. For this reason, appropriately, I had come as the skull and the eye to Costabel—the coast demanding shipwreck. Why else had I remembered the phrase, except for a dark impulse toward destruction lurking somewhere in the subconscious? I lay on the bed while the agonized eye in the remembered photograph persisted at the back of my closed lids.

It had begun when, after years of separation, I had gone dutifully home to a house from which the final occupant had departed. In a musty attic—among old trunks, a broken aquarium, and a dusty heap of fossil shells collected in childhood—I found a satchel. The satchel was already a shabby antique, in whose depths I turned up a jackknife and a "rat" of hair such as women wore at the beginning of the century. Beneath these lay a pile of old photographs and a note—two notes, rather, evidently dropped into the bag at different times. Each, in a thin, ornate hand, reiterated a single message that the writer had believed important. "This satchel belongs to my son, Loren Eiseley." It was the last message. I recognized the trivia. The jackknife I had carried in childhood. The rat of hair had belonged to my mother, and there were also two incredibly pointed slippers that looked as though they had been intended for a formal ball, to which I knew well my mother would never in her life have been invited. I undid the rotted string around the studio portraits.

Mostly they consisted of stiff, upright bearded men and heavily clothed women equally bound to the formalities and ritual that attended upon the photography of an earlier generation. No names identified the pictures, although here and there a reminiscent family trait seemed faintly evident. Finally I came upon a less formal photograph, taken in the eighties of the last century. Again no names iden-tified the people, but a commercial stamp upon the back identified the place: Dyersville, Iowa. I had never been in that country town, but I knew at once it was my mother's birthplace.

Dyersville, the thought flashed through my mind, making the con-nection now for the first time: the dire place. I recognized at once the two sisters at the edge of the photograph, the younger clinging reluc-tantly to the older. Six years old, I thought, turning momentarily away from the younger child's face. Here it began, her pain and mine. The eyes in the photograph were already remote and shadowed by some inner turmoil. The poise of the body was already that of one miserably departing the peripheries of the human estate. The gaze was mutely clairvoyant and lonely. It was the gaze of a child who knew unbearable difference and impending isolation.

I dropped the notes and pictures once more into the bag. The last message had come from Dyersville: "my son." The child in the photo-graph had survived to be an ill-taught prairie artist. She had been deaf. All her life she had walked the precipice of mental breakdown. Here on this faded porch it had begun—the long crucifixion of life. I slipped downstairs and out of the house. I walked for miles through the streets.

Now at Costabel I put on the sunglasses once more, but the face from the torn photograph persisted behind them. It was as though I, as man, was being asked to confront, in all its overbearing weight, the universe itself. "Love not the world," the Biblical injunction runs, "nei-ther the things that are in the world." The revolving beam in my mind had stopped, and the insect whisperings of the intellect. There was, at last, an utter stillness, a waiting as though for a cosmic judgment. The eye, the torn eye, considered me.

"But I *do* love the world," I whispered to a waiting presence in the empty room. "I love its small ones, the things beaten in the strangling surf, the bird, singing, which flies and falls and is not seen again." I choked and said, with the torn eye still upon me, "I love the lost ones, the failures of the world." It was like the renunciation of my scientific heritage. The torn eye surveyed me sadly and was gone. I had come full upon one of the last great rifts in nature, and the merciless beam no longer was in traverse around my skull.

But no, it was not a rift but a joining: the expression of love projected beyond the species boundary by a creature born of Darwinian struggle, in the silent war under the tangled bank. "There is no boon in nature," one of the new philosophers had written harshly in the first years of the industrial cities. Nevertheless, through war and famine and death, a sparse mercy had persisted, like a mutation whose time had not yet come. I had seen the star thrower cross that rift and, in so doing, he had reasserted the human right to define his own frontier. He had moved to the utmost edge of natural being, if not across its boundaries. It was as though at some point the supernatural had touched hesitantly, for an instant, upon the natural.

Out of the depths of a seemingly empty universe had grown an eye, like the eye in my room, but an eye on a vastly larger scale. It looked out upon what I can only call itself. It searched the skies and it searched the depths of being. In the shape of man it had ascended like a vaporous emanation from the depths of night. The nothing had miraculously gazed upon the nothing and was not content. It was an intrusion into, or a projection out of, nature for which no precedent existed. The act was, in short, an assertion of value arisen from the domain of absolute zero. A little whirlwind of commingling molecules had succeeded in confronting its own universe.

Here, at last, was the rift that lay beyond Darwin's tangled bank. For a creature, arisen from that bank and born of its contentions, had stretched out its hand in pity. Some ancient, inexhaustible, and patient intelligence, lying dispersed in the planetary fields of force or amidst the inconceivable cold of interstellar space, had chosen to endow its desolation with an apparition as mysterious as itself. The fate of man is to be the ever recurrent, reproachful Eye floating upon night and solitude. The world cannot be said to exist save by the interposition of that inward eye—an eye various and not under the restraints to be apprehended from what is vulgarly called the natural.

I had been unbelieving. I had walked away from the star thrower in the hardened indifference of maturity. But thought mediated by the eye is one of nature's infinite disguises. Belatedly, I arose with a solitary mission. I set forth in an effort to find the star thrower.

IV

Man is himself, like the universe he inhabits, like the demoniacal stirrings of the ooze from which he sprang, a tale of desolations. He walks in his mind from birth to death the long resounding shores of endless disillusionment. Finally, the commitment to life departs or turns to bitterness. But out of such desolation emerges the awesome freedom to choose—to choose beyond the narrowly circumscribed circle that delimits the animal being. In that widening ring of human choice, chaos and order renew their symbolic struggle in the role of titans. They contend for the destiny of a world.

Somewhere far up the coast wandered the star thrower beneath his rainbow. Our exchange had been brief because upon that coast I had learned that men who ventured out at dawn resented others in the greediness of their compulsive collecting. I had also been abrupt because I had, in the terms of my profession and experience, nothing to say. The star thrower was mad, and his particular acts were a folly with which I had not chosen to associate myself. I was an observer and a scientist. Nevertheless, I had seen the rainbow attempting to attach itself to earth.

On a point of land, as though projecting into a domain beyond us, I found the star thrower. In the sweet rain-swept morning, that great many-hued rainbow still lurked and wavered tentatively beyond him.

Silently I sought and picked up a still-living star, spinning it far out into the waves. I spoke once briefly. "I understand," I said. "Call me another thrower." Only then I allowed myself to think, He is not alone any longer. After us there will be others.

We were part of the rainbow—an unexplained projection into the natural. As I went down the beach I could feel the drawing of a circle in men's minds, like that lowering, shifting realm of color in which the thrower labored. It was a visible model of something toward which man's mind had striven, the circle of perfection.

I picked and flung another star. Perhaps far outward on the rim of space a genuine star was similarly seized and flung. I could feel the movement in my body. It was like a sowing—the sowing of life on an infinitely gigantic scale. I looked back across my shoulder. Small and dark against the receding rainbow, the star thrower stooped and flung once more. I never looked again. The task we had assumed was too immense for gazing. I flung and flung again while all about us roared the insatiable waters of death.

But we, pale and alone and small in that immensity, hurled back the living stars. Somewhere far off, across bottomless abysses, I felt as though another world was flung more joyfully. I could have thrown in a frenzy of joy, but I set my shoulders and cast, as the thrower in the rainbow cast, slowly, deliberately, and well. The task was not to be assumed lightly, for it was men as well as starfish that we sought to save. For a moment, we cast on an infinite beach together beside an unknown hurler of suns. It was, unsought, the destiny of my kind since the rituals of the ice age hunters, when life in the Northern Hemisphere had come close to vanishing. We had lost our way, I thought, but we had kept, some of us, the memory of the perfect circle of compassion from life to death and back again to life—the completion of the rainbow of existence. Even the hunters in the snow, making obeisance to the souls of the hunted, had known the cycle. The legend had come down and lingered that he who gained the gratitude of animals gained help in need from the dark wood.

I cast again with an increasingly remembered sowing motion and went my lone way up the beaches. Somewhere, I felt, in a great atavistic surge of feeling, somewhere the Thrower knew. Perhaps he smiled and cast once more into the boundless pit of darkness. Perhaps he, too, was lonely, and the end toward which he labored remained hidden—even as with ourselves.

I picked up a star whose tube feet ventured timidly among my fingers while, like a true star, it cried soundlessly for life. I saw it with an unaccustomed clarity and cast far out. With it, I flung myself as forfeit, for the first time, into some unknown dimension of existence. From Darwin's tangled bank of unceasing struggle, selfishness, and death, had arisen, incomprehensibly, the thrower who loved not man, but life. It was the subtle cleft in nature before which biological thinking had faltered. We had reached the last shore of an invisible island—yet, strangely, also a shore that the primitives had always known. They had sensed intuitively that man cannot exist spiritually without life, his brother, even if he slays. Somewhere, my thought persisted, there is a hurler of stars, and he walks, because he chooses, always in desolation, but not in defeat.

In the night the gas flames under the shelling kettles would continue to glow. I set my clock accordingly. Tomorrow I would walk in the storm. I would walk against the shell collectors and the flames. I would walk remembering Bacon's forgotten words "for the uses of life." I would walk with the knowledge of the discontinuities of the unexpected universe. I would walk knowing of the rift revealed by the thrower, a hint that there looms, inexplicably, in nature something above the role men give her. I knew it from the man at the foot of the rainbow, the starfish thrower on the beaches of Costabel.

The Last Neanderthal

For thou shalt be in league with the stones of the field:
and the beasts of the field shall be at peace with thee.

JOB 5:23

It has long been the thought of science, particularly in evolutionary biology, that nature does not make extended leaps, that her creatures slip in slow disguise from one shape to another. A simple observation will reveal, however, that there are rocks in deserts that glow with heat for a time after sundown. Similar emanations may come from the writer or the scientist. The creative individual is someone upon whom mysterious rays have converged and are again reflected, not necessarily immediately, but in the course of years. That all of this wispy geometry of dreams and memories should be the product of a kind of slow-burning oxidation carried on in an equally diffuse and mediating web of nerve and sense cells is surprising enough, but that the emanations from the same particulate organ, the brain, should be so strikingly different as to disobey the old truism of an unleaping nature is quite surprising, once one comes to contemplate the reality.

The same incident may stand as a simple fact to some, an intangible hint of the nature of the universe to others, a useful myth to a savage, or any number of other things. The receptive mind makes all the difference, shadowing or lighting the original object. I was an observer, intent upon my own solitary hieroglyphics.

It happened a long time ago at Curaçao, in the Netherlands Antilles, on a shore marked by the exposed ribs of a wrecked freighter. The place was one where only a student of desolation would find cause to linger. Pelicans perched awkwardly on what remained of a rusted prow. On the edge of the littered beach beyond the port I had come upon a dead dog wrapped in burlap, obviously buried at sea and drifted in by the waves. The dog was little more than a skeleton but still articulated, one delicate bony paw laid gracefully—as though its owner merely slept, and would presently awaken—across a stone at the water's edge. Around his throat was a waterlogged black strap that showed he had once belonged to someone. This dog was a mongrel whose life had been spent among the island fishermen. He had known only the small sea-beaten boats that come across the strait from Venezuela. He had romped briefly on shores like this to which he had been returned by the indifferent sea.

I stepped back a little hesitantly from the smell of death, but still I paused reluctantly. Why, in this cove littered with tin cans, bottles, and cast-off garments, did I find it difficult, if not a sacrilege, to turn away? Because, the thought finally came to me, this particular tattered garment had once lived. Scenes on the living sea that would never in all eternity recur again had streamed through the sockets of those vanished eyes. The dog was young, the teeth in its jaws still perfect. It was of that type of loving creature who had gamboled happily about the legs of men and striven to partake of their endeavors.

Someone had seen crudely to his sea burial, but not well enough to prevent his lying now where came everything abandoned. Nevertheless, vast natural forces had intervened to clothe him with a pathetic dignity. The tide had brought him quietly at night and placed what remained of him asleep upon the stones. Here at sunrise I had stood above him in a light he would never any longer see. Even if I had had a shovel the stones would have prevented his burial. He would wait for a second tide to spirit him away or lay him higher to bleach starkly upon coral and conch shells, mingling the little lime of his bones with all else that had once stood upright on these shores.

As I turned upward into the hills beyond the beach I was faintly aware of a tracery of lizard tails amidst the sand and the semidesert shrubbery. The lizards were so numerous on the desert floor that their swift movement in the bright sun left a dizzying impression, like spots dancing before one's eyes. The creatures had a tangential way of darting off to the side like inconsequential thoughts that never paused long enough to be fully apprehended. One's eyesight was oppressed by subtly moving points where all should have been quiet. Similar darting specks seemed to be invading my mind. Offshore I could hear the sea wheezing and suspiring in long gasps among the caverns of the coral. The equatorial sun blazed on my unprotected head and hummingbirds flashed like little green flames in the underbrush. I sought quick shelter under a manzanillo tree, whose poisoned apples had tempted the sailors of Columbus.

I suppose the apples really made the connection. Or perhaps merely the interior rustling of the lizards, as I passed some cardboard boxes beside a fence, brought the thing to mind. Or again, it may have been the tropic sun, lending its flames to life with a kind of dreadful indifference as to the result. At any rate, as I shielded my head under the leaves of the poison tree, the darting lizard points began to run together into a pattern.

Before me passed a broken old horse plodding before a cart laden with bags of cast-off clothing, discarded furniture, and abandoned metal. The horse's harness was a makeshift combination of straps mended with rope. The bearded man perched high in the driver's seat looked as though he had been compounded from the assorted junk heap in the wagon bed. What finally occupied the center of my attention, however, was a street sign and a year—a year that scurried into shape with the flickering alacrity of the lizards. "R Street," they spelled, and the year was 1923.

By now the man on the wagon is dead, his cargo dispersed, never to be reassembled. The plodding beast has been overtaken by whatever fate comes upon a junkman's horse. Their significance upon that particular day in 1923 had been resolved to this, just this: The wagon had been passing the intersection between R and Fourteenth streets when I had leaned from a high-school window a block away, absorbed as only a sixteen-year-old may sometimes be with the sudden discovery of time. It is all going, I thought with the bitter desperation of the young confronting history. No one can hold us. Each and all, we are riding into the dark. Even living, we cannot remember half the events of our own days.

At that moment my eye had fallen upon the junk dealer passing his fateful corner. Now, I had thought instantly, now, save him, immortalize the unseizable moment. The junkman is the symbol of all that is going or is gone. He is passing the intersection into nothingness. Say to the mind, "Hold him, do not forget."

The darting lizard points beyond the manzanillo tree converged and tightened. The phantom horse and the heaped, chaotic wagon were still jouncing across the intersection upon R Street. They had never crossed it; they would not. Forty-five years had fled away. I was not wrong about the powers latent in the brain. The scene was still in process.

I estimated the lowering of the sun with one eye while at the back of my mind the lizard rustling continued. The blistering apples of the manzanillo reminded me of an inconsequential wild-plum fall far away in Nebraska. They were not edible but they contained the same, if a simpler, version of the mystery hidden in our heads. They were hoarding and dispersing energy while the inanimate universe was running down around us.

"We must regard the organism as a configuration contrived to evade the tendency of the universal laws of nature," John Joly the geologist had once remarked. Unlike the fire in a thicket, life burned cunningly and hoarded its resources. Energy provisions in the seed provided against individual death. Of all the unexpected qualities of an unexpected universe, the sheer organizing power of animal and plant metabolism is one of the most remarkable, but, as in the case of most everyday marvels, we take it for granted. Where it reaches its highest development, in the human mind, we forget it completely. Yet out of it history is made—the junkman on R Street is prevented from departing. Growing increasingly archaic, that phantom would be held at the R Street intersection while all around him new houses arose and the years passed unremembered. He would not be released until my own mind began to crumble.

The power to free him is not mine. He is held enchanted because long ago I willed a miniature of history, confined to a single brain. That brain is devouring oxygen at a rate out of all proportion to the rest of the body. It is involved in burning, evoking, and transposing visions, whether of lizard tails, alphabets from the sea, or the realms beyond the galaxy. So important does nature regard this unseen combustion, this smoke of the planet's autumn, that a starving man's brain will be protected to the last while his body is steadily consumed. It is a part of unexpected nature.

In the rational universe of the physical laboratory this sullen and obstinate burning might not, save for our habit of taking the existent for granted, have been expected. Nonetheless, it is here, and man is its most tremendous manifestation. One might ask, Would it be possible to understand humanity a little better if one could follow along just a step of the evolutionary pathway in person? Suppose that there still lived ... but let me tell the tale, make of it what you will.

II

Years after the experience of which I am about to speak, I came upon a recent but Neanderthaloid skull in the dissecting room—a rare enough occurrence, one that the far-out flitting of forgotten genes struggles occasionally to produce, as if life sometimes hesitated and were inclined to turn back upon its pathway. For a time, remembering an episode of my youth, I kept the indices of cranial measurement by me.

Today, thinking of that experience, I have searched vainly for my old notebook. It is gone. The years have a way of caring for things that do not seek the safety of print. The earlier event remains, however, because it was not a matter of measurements or anthropological indices but of a living person whom I once knew. Now, in my autumn, the face of that girl and the strange season I spent in her neighborhood return in a kind of hazy lesson that I was too young to understand.

It happened in the West, somewhere in that wide drought-ridden land of empty coulees that carry in sudden spates of flood the boulders of the Rockies toward the sea. I suppose that, with the outward flight of population, the region is as wild now as it was then, some forty years ago. It would be useless to search for the place upon a map, though I have tried. Too many years and too many uncertain miles lie behind all bone hunters. There was no town to fix upon a road map. There was only a sod house tucked behind a butte, out of the prevailing wind. And there was a little spring-fed pond in a grassy meadow—that I remember.

Bone hunting is not really a very romantic occupation. One walks day after day along miles of frequently unrewarding outcrop. One grows browner, leaner, and tougher, it is true, but one is far from the bright lights, and the prospect, barring a big strike, like a mammoth, is always to abandon camp and go on. It was really a gypsy profession, then, for those who did the field collecting.

In this case, we did not go on. There was an eroding hill in the vicinity, and on top of that hill, just below sod cover, were the foot bones, hundreds of them, of some lost Tertiary species of American rhinoceros. It is useless to ask why we found only foot bones or why we gathered the mineralized things in such fantastic quantities that they must still lie stacked in some museum storeroom. Maybe the creatures had been immured standing up in a waterhole and in the millions of succeeding years the rest of the carcasses had eroded away from the hilltop stratum. But there were the foot bones, and the orders had come down, so we dug carpals and metacarpals till we cursed like an army platoon that headquarters has forgotten.

There was just one diversion: the spring, and the pond in the meadow. There, under the bank, we cooled our milk and butter purchased from the soddy inhabitants. There we swam and splashed after work. The country people were reserved and kept mostly to themselves. They were uninterested in the dull bones on the hilltop unenlivened by skulls or treasure. After all, there was reason for their reserve. We must have appeared, by their rural standards, harmless but undoubtedly touched in the head. The barrier of reserve was never broken. The surly farmer kept to his parched acres and estimated to his profit our damage to his uncultivated hilltop. The slatternly wife tended a few scrawny chickens. In that ever blowing landscape their windmill largely ran itself.

Only a stocky barefoot girl of twenty sometimes came hesitantly down the path to our camp to deliver eggs. Some sixty days had drifted by upon that hillside. I began to remember the remark of an old fossil hunter who in his time had known the Gold Coast and the African veldt. "When calico begins to look like silk," he had once warned over a fire in the Sierras, "it is time to go home."

But enough of that. We were not bad young people. The girl shyly brought us the eggs, the butter, and the bacon, and then withdrew. Only after some little time did her appearance begin to strike me as odd. Men are accustomed to men in their various color variations around the world. When the past intrudes into a modern setting, however, it is less apt to be visible, because to see it demands knowledge of the past, and the past is always camouflaged when it wears the clothes of the present.

The girl came slowly down the trail one evening, and it struck me suddenly how alone she looked and how, well, *alien,* she also appeared. Our cook was stoking up the evening fire, and as the shadows leaped and flickered I, leaning invisibly against a rock, was suddenly transported one hundred thousand years into the past. The shadows and their dancing highlights were the cause of it. They had swept the present out of sight. That girl coming reluctantly down the pathway to the fire was removed from us in time, and subconsciously she knew it as I did. By modern standards she was not pretty, and the gingham dress she wore, if anything, defined the difference.

Short, thickset, and massive, her body was still not the body of a typical peasant woman. Her head, thrust a little forward against the light, was massive-boned. Along the eye orbits at the edge of the frontal bone I could see outlined in the flames an armored protuberance that, particularly in women, had vanished before the close of the Würmian ice. She swung her head almost like a great muzzle beneath its curls, and I was struck by the low bun-shaped breadth at the back. Along her exposed arms one could see a flash of golden hair.

No, we are out of time, I thought quickly. We are each and every one displaced. She is the last Neanderthal, and she does not know what to do. We are those who eliminated her long ago. It is like an old scene endlessly re-enacted. Only the chipped stones and the dead game are lacking.

I came out of the shadow then and spoke gently to her, taking the packages. It was the most one could do across that waste of infinite years. She spoke almost inaudibly, drawing an unconscious circle in the dust with a splayed bare foot. I saw, through the thin dress, the powerful thighs, the yearning fertility going unmated in this lonesome spot. She looked up, and a trick of the fire accentuated the cavernous eye sockets so that I saw only darkness within. I accompanied her a short distance along the trail. "What is it you are digging for?" she managed to ask.

"It has to do with time," I said slowly. "Something that happened a long time ago."

She listened incuriously, as one at the morning of creation might do.

"Do you like this?" she persisted. "Do you always just go from one place to another digging these things? And who pays for it, and what comes of it in the end? Do you have a home?" The soddy and her burly father were looming in the dusk. I paused, but questions flung across the centuries are hard to answer.

"I am a student," I said, but with no confidence. How could I say that suddenly she herself and her ulnar-bowed and golden-haired forearms were a part of a long reach backward into time?

"Of what has been, and what will come of it we are trying to find out. I am afraid it will not help one to find a home," I said, more to myself than her. "Quite the reverse, in fact. You see—"

The dark sockets under the tumbled hair seemed somehow sadly vacant. "Thank you for bringing the things," I said, knowing the customs of that land. "Your father is waiting. I will go back to camp now." With this I strode off toward our fire but went, on impulse, beyond it into the full-starred night.

This was the way of things along the Wild Cat escarpment. There was sand blowing and the past mingling with the present in more ways than professional science chose to see. There were eroded farms no longer running cattle and a diminishing population waiting, as this girl was waiting, for something they would never possess. They were, without realizing it, huntsmen without game, women without warriors. Obsolescence was upon their way of life.

But about the girl lingered a curious gentleness that we know now had long ago touched the vanished Neanderthals she so resembled. It would be her fate to marry eventually one of the illiterate hard-eyed uplanders of my own kind. Whatever the subtle genes had resurrected in her body would be buried once more and hidden in the creature called *sapiens*. Perhaps in the end his last woman would stand unwanted before some fiercer, brighter version of himself. It would be no more than justice. I was farther out in the deep spaces than I knew, and the fire was embers when I returned.

The season was waning. There came, inevitably, a time when the trees began to talk of winter in the crags above the camp. I have repeated all that can be said about so fragile an episode. I had exchanged in the course of weeks a few wistful, scarcely understood remarks. I had waved to her a time or so from the quarry hilltop. As the time of our departure neared I had once glimpsed her shyly surveying from a rise beyond the pond our youthful plungings and naked wallowings in the spring-fed water. Then suddenly the leaves were down or turning yellow. It was time to go. The fossil quarry and its interminable foot bones were at last exhausted.

But something never intended had arisen for me there by the darkening water—some agonizing, lifelong nostalgia, both personal and, in another sense, transcending the personal. It was—how shall I say it?—the endurance in a single mind of two stages of man's climb up the energy ladder that may be both his triumph and his doom.

Our battered equipment was assembled in the Model T's, which, in that time, were the only penetrators of deep-rutted upland roads. Morose good-byes were expressed; money was passed over the broken sod cover on the hilltop. Hundreds of once galloping rhinoceros foot bones were stowed safely away. And that was it. I stood by the running board and slowly, very slowly, let my eyes wander toward that massive, archaic, and yet tragically noble head—of a creature so far back in time it did not know it represented tragedy. I made, I think, some kind of little personal gesture of farewell. Her head raised in recognition and then dropped. The motors started. *Homo sapiens,* the energy devourer, was on his way once more.

What was it she had said, I thought desperately as I swung aboard. Home, she had questioned, "Do you have a home?" Perhaps I once did, I was to think many times in the years that followed, but I, too, was a mental atavism. I, like that lost creature, would never find the place called home. It lay somewhere in the past down that hundred-thousand-year road on which travel was impossible. Only ghosts with uncertain eyes and abashed gestures would meet there. Upon a surging tide of power first conceived in the hearth fires of dead caverns mankind was plunging into an uncontrolled future beyond anything the people of the Ice had known.

The cell that had somehow mastered the secret of controlled energy, of surreptitious burning to a purpose, had finally produced the mind, judiciously, in its turn, controlling the inconstant fire at the cave mouth. Beyond anything that lost girl could imagine, words in the mouth or immured in libraries would cause substance to vanish and the earth itself to tremble. The little increments of individual energy dissolving at death had been coded and passed through the centuries by human ingenuity. A climbing juggernaut of power was leaping from triumph to triumph. It threatened to be more than man and all his words could master. It was more and less than man.

I remembered those cavernous eye sockets whose depths were forever hidden from me in the firelight. Did they contain a premonition of the end we had invited, or was it only that I was young and hungry for all that was untouchable? I have searched once more for the old notebooks but, again, in vain. They would tell me, at best, only how living phantoms can be anatomically compared with those of the past. They would tell nothing of that season of the falling leaves or how I learned under the night sky of the utter homelessness of man.

III

I have seen a tree root burst a rock face on a mountain or slowly wrench aside the gateway of a forgotten city. This is a very cunning feat, which men take too readily for granted. Life, unlike the inanimate, will take the long way round to circumvent barrenness. A kind of desperate will resides even in a root. It will perform the evasive tactics of an army, slowly inching its way through crevices and hoarding energy until someday it swells and a living tree upheaves the heaviest mausoleum. This covert struggle is part of the lifelong battle waged against the Second Law of Thermodynamics, the heat death that has been frequently assumed to rule the universe. At the hands of man that hoarded energy takes strange forms, both in the methods of its accumulation and in the diverse ways of its expenditure.

For hundreds of thousands of years, a time longer than all we know of recorded history, the kin of that phantom girl had lived without cities along the Italian Mediterranean or below the northern tentacles of the groping ice. The low archaic skull vault had been as capacious as ours. Neanderthal man had, we now know after long digging, his own small dreams and kindnesses. He had buried his dead with offerings—there were even evidences that they had been laid, in some instances, upon beds of wild flowers. Beyond the chipped flints and the fires in the cavern darkness his mind had not involved itself with what was to come upon him with our kind—the first bowmen, the great artists, the terrible creatures of his blood who were never still.

It was a time of autumn driftage that might have lasted and been well forever. Whether it was his own heavy brow that changed in the chill nights or that somewhere his line had mingled with a changeling cuckoo brood who multiplied at his expense we do not know with certainty. We know only that he vanished, though sometimes, as in the case of my upland girl, a chance assemblage of archaic genes struggles to reemerge from the loins of *sapiens*.

But the plucked flint had flown; the heavy sad girls had borne the children of the conquerors. Rain and leaves washed over the cave shelters of the past. Bronze replaced flint, iron replaced bronze, while the killing never ceased. The Neanderthals were forgotten; their grottoes housed the oracles of later religions. Marble cities gleamed along the Mediterranean. The ice and the cave bear had vanished. White-robed philosophers discoursed in Athens. Armed galleys moved upon the waters. Agriculture had brought wealth and diversification of labor. It had also brought professional soldiery. The armored ones were growing and, with them, slavery, torture, and death upon all the seas of the world.

The energy that had once sufficed only to take man from one camping place to another, the harsh but innocent world glimpsed by Cook in the eighteenth century on the shores of Australia, century by century was driving toward a climax. The warriors with the tall foreheads given increasingly to fanatic religions and monumental art had finally grown to doubt the creations of their own minds.

The remnants of what had once been talked about in Athens and been consumed in the flames of Alexandria hesitantly crept forth once more. Early in the seventeenth century Sir Francis Bacon asserted that "by the agency of man a new aspect of things, a new universe, comes into view." In those words he was laying the basis of what he came to call "the second world," that world which could be drawn out of the natural by the sheer power of the human mind. Man had, of course, unwittingly been doing something of the sort since he came to speak. Bacon, however, was dreaming of the new world of invention, of toleration, of escape from irrational custom. He was the herald of the scientific method itself. Yet that method demands history also—the history I as an eager student had long ago beheld symbolically upon a corner in the shape of a junkman's cart. Without knowledge of the past, the way into the thickets of the future is desperate and unclear.

Bacon's second world is now so much with us that it rocks our conception of what the natural order was, or is, or in what sense it can be restored. A mathematical formula traveling weakly along the fibers of the neopallium may serve to wreck the planet. It is a kind of metabolic energy never envisaged by the lichen attacking a rock face or dreamed of in the flickering shadows of a cave fire. Yet from these ancient sources man's hunger has been drawn. Its potential is to be found in the life of the world we call natural, just as its terrifying intricacy is the product of the second visionary world evoked in the brain of man.

The two exist on the planet in an increasingly uneven balance. Into one or the other or into a terrifying nothing one of these two worlds must finally subside. Man, whose strange metabolism has passed beyond the search for food to the naked ingestion of power, is scarcely aware that the energy whose limited planetary store lies at the root of the struggle for existence has passed by way of his mind into another dimension. There the giant shadows of the past continue to contend. They do so because life is a furnace of concealed flame.

Some pages back I spoke of a wild-plum thicket. I did so because I had a youthful memory of visiting it in autumn. All the hoarded juices of summer had fallen with that lush untasted fruit upon the grass. The tiny engines of the plant had painstakingly gathered throughout the summer rich stores of sugar and syrup from the ground. Seed had been produced; birds had flown away with fruit that would give rise to plum trees miles away. The energy dispersion was so beneficent on that autumn afternoon that earth itself seemed anxious to promote the process against the downward guttering of the stars. Even I, tasting the fruit, was in my animal way scooping up some of it into thoughts and dreams.

Long after the Antillean adventure I chanced on an autumn walk to revisit the plum thicket. I was older, much older, and I had come largely because I wondered if the thicket was still there and because this strange hoarding and burning at the heart of life still puzzled me.

I have spoken figuratively of fire as an animal, as being perhaps the very *essence* of animal. Oxidation, I mean, as it enters into life and consciousness.

Fire, as we have learned to our cost, has an insatiable hunger to be fed. It is a nonliving force that can even locomote itself. What if now— and I half closed my eyes against the blue plums and the smoke drifting along the draw—what if now it is only concealed and grown slyly conscious of its own burning in this little house of sticks and clay that I inhabit? What if I am, in some way, only a sophisticated fire that has acquired an ability to regulate its rate of combustion and to hoard its fuel in order to see and walk?

The plums, like some gift given from no one to no one visible, continued to fall about me. I was old now, I thought suddenly, glancing at a vein on my hand. I would have to hoard what remained of the embers. I thought of the junkman's horse and tried to release him so that he might be gone.

Perhaps I had finally succeeded. I do not know. I remembered that star-filled night years ago on the escarpment and the heavy-headed dreaming girl drawing a circle in the dust. Perhaps it was time itself she drew, for my own head was growing heavy and the smoke from the autumn fields seemed to be penetrating my mind. I wanted to drop them at last, these carefully hoarded memories. I wanted to strew them like the blue plums in some gesture of love toward the universe all outward on a mat of leaves. Rich, rich and not to be hoarded, only to be laid down for someone, anyone, no longer to be carried and remembered in pain like the delicate paw lying forever on the beach at Curaçao.

I leaned farther back, relaxing in the leaves. It was a feeling I had never had before, and it was strangely soothing. Perhaps I was no longer *Homo sapiens,* and perhaps that girl, the last Neanderthal, had known as much from the first. Perhaps all I was, really, was a pile of autumn leaves seeing smoke wraiths through the haze of my own burning. Things get odder on this planet, not less so. I dropped my head finally and gazed straight up through the branches at the sun. It was all going, I felt, memories dropping away in that high indifferent blaze that tolerated no other light. I let it be so for a little, but then I felt in my pocket the flint blade that I had carried all those years from the gravels on the escarpment. It reminded me of a journey I would not complete and the circle in the dust around which I had magically traveled for so long.

I arose then and, biting a plum that tasted bitter, I limped off down the ravine. One hundred thousand years had made little difference— at least, to me. The secret was to travel always in the first world, not the second; or, at least, to know at each crossroad which world was which. I went on, clutching for stability the flint knife in my pocket. A blue smoke like some final conflagration swept out of the draw and preceded me. I could feel its heat. I coughed, and my eyes watered. I tried as best I could to keep pace with it as it swirled on. There was a crackling behind me as though I myself were burning, but the smoke was what I followed. I held the sharp flint like a dowser's twig, cold and steady in my hand.

.

The Innocent Fox

Only to a magician is the world forever fluid,
infinitely mutable and eternally new. Only he
knows the secret of change, only he knows
truly that all things are crouched in eagerness
to become something else, and it is from this
universal tension that he draws his power.

PETER BEAGLE

Since man first saw an impossible visage staring upward from a still pool, he has been haunted by meanings—meanings felt even in the wood, where the trees leaned over him, manifesting a vast and living presence. The image in the pool vanished at the touch of his finger, but he went home and created a legend. The great trees never spoke, but man knew that dryads slipped among their boles. Since the red morning of time it has been so, and the compulsive reading of such manuscripts will continue to occupy man's attention long after the books that contain his inmost thoughts have been sealed away by the indefatigable spider.

Some men are daylight readers, who peruse the ambiguous wording of clouds or the individual letter shapes of wandering birds. Some, like myself, are librarians of the night, whose ephemeral documents consist of root-inscribed bones or whatever rustles in thickets upon solitary walks. Man, for all his daylight activities, is, at best, an evening creature. Our very addiction to the day and our compulsion, manifest through the ages, to invent and use illuminating devices, to contest with midnight, to cast off sleep as we would death, suggest that we know more of the shadows than we are willing to recognize. We have come from the dark wood of the past, and our bodies carry the scars and unhealed wounds of that transition. Our minds are haunted by night terrors that arise from the subterranean domain of racial and private memories.

Lastly, we inhabit a spiritual twilight on this planet. It is perhaps the most poignant of all the deprivations to which man has been exposed by nature. I have said *deprivation*, but perhaps I should, rather, maintain that this feeling of loss is an unrealized anticipation. We imagine we are day creatures, but we grope in a lawless and smoky realm toward an exit that eludes us. We appear to know instinctively that such an exit exists.

I am not the first man to have lost his way only to find, if not a gate, a mysterious hole in a hedge that a child would know at once led to some other dimension at the world's end. Such passageways exist, or man would not be here. Not for nothing did Santayana once contend that life is a movement from the forgotten into the unexpected.

As adults, we are preoccupied with living. As a consequence, we see little. At the approach of age some men look about them at last and discover the hole in the hedge leading to the unforeseen. By then, there is frequently no child companion to lead them safely through. After one or two experiences of getting impaled on thorns, the most persistent individual is apt to withdraw and to assert angrily that no such opening exists.

My experience has been quite the opposite, but I have been fortunate. After several unsuccessful but tantalizing trials, which I intend to disclose, I had the help, not of a child, but of a creature—a creature who, appropriately, came out of a quite unremarkable and prosaic den.

There was nothing, in retrospect, at all mysterious or unreal about him. Nevertheless, the creature was baffling, just as, I suppose, to animals, man himself is baffling.

II

An autumn midnight in 1967 caught me staring idly from my study window at the attic cupola of an old Victorian house that loomed far above a neighboring grove of trees. I suppose the episode happened just as I had grown dimly aware, amidst my encasing cocoon of books and papers, that something was missing from my life. This feeling had brought me from my desk to peer hopelessly upon the relentless advance of suburban housing. For years, I had not seen anything from that particular window that did not spell the death of something I loved.

Finally, in blundering, good-natured confidence, the last land tortoise had fallen a victim to the new expressway. None of his kind any longer came to replace him. A chipmunk that had held out valiantly in a drainpipe on the lawn had been forced to flee from the usurping rats that had come with the new supermarket. A parking lot now occupied most of the view from the window. I was a man trapped in the despair once alluded to as the utterly hopeless fear confined to moderns—that no miracles can ever happen. I considered, as I tried to will myself away into the attic room far above the trees, the wisdom of a search, a search unlikely to yield tangible results.

Since boyhood I have been charmed by the unexpected and the beautiful. This was what had led me originally into science, but now I felt instinctively that something more was needed—though what I needed verged on a miracle. As a scientist, I did not believe in miracles, though I willingly granted the word broad latitudes of definition.

My whole life had been unconsciously a search, and the search had not been restricted to the bones and stones of my visible profession.

Moreover, my age could allow me folly; indeed, it demanded a boldness that the young frequently cannot afford. All I needed to do was to set forth either mentally or physically, but to where escaped me.

At that instant the high dormer window beyond the trees blazed as blue as a lightning flash. As I have remarked, it was midnight. There was no possibility of reflection from a street lamp. A giant bolt of artificial lightning was playing from a condenser, leaping at intervals across the interior of the black pane in the distance. It was the artificial lightning that only one or several engineers with unusual equipment could produce.

Now the old house was plebeian enough. Rooms were rented. People of modest middle-class means lived there, as I was to learn later. But still, in the midmost of the night, somebody or some group was engaged in that attic room upon a fantastic experiment. For, you see, I spied. I spied for nights in succession. I was bored, I was sleepless, and it pleased me to think that the mad scientists, as I came to call them, were engaged, in their hidden room, upon some remarkable and unheard-of adventure.

Why else would they be active at midnight, why else would they be engaged for a brief hour and then extinguish the spark? In the next few days I trained high-powered field glasses upon the window, but the blue bolt defeated me, as did the wavering of autumn boughs across the distant roof. I could only believe that science still possessed some of its old, mad fascination for a mind outside the professional circle of the great laboratories. Perhaps, I thought eagerly, there was a fresh intelligence groping after some secret beyond pure technology. I thought of the dreams of Emerson and others when evolution was first anticipated but its mechanisms remained a mystery entangled with the first galvanic batteries. Night after night, while the leaves thinned and the bolt leaped at its appointed hour, I dreamed, staring from my window, of that coruscating arc revivifying flesh or leaping sentient beyond it into some unguessed state of being. Only for such purposes, I thought, would a man toil in an attic room at midnight.

I began unconsciously to hang more and more upon that work of which, in reality, I knew nothing. It sustained me in my waking hours when the old house, amidst its yellowing leaves, assumed a sleepy and inconsequential air. For me, it had restored wonder and lifted my dreams to the height they had once had when, as a young student, I had peeped through the glass door of a famous experimenter's laboratory. I no longer read. I sat in the darkened study and watched and waited for the unforeseen. It came in a way I had not expected.

One night the window remained dark. My powerful glasses revealed only birds flying across the face of the moon. A bat fluttered about the tessellated chimney. A few remaining leaves fell into the dark below the roofs.

I waited expectantly for the experiment to be resumed. It was not. The next night it rained violently. The window did not glow. Leaves yellowed the wet walks below the street lamps. It was the same the next night and the next. The episode, I came to feel, peering ruefully from my window, was altogether too much like science itself—science with its lightning bolts, its bubbling retorts, its elusive promises of perfection. All too frequently the dream ended in a downpour of rain and leaves upon wet walks. The men involved had a way, like my mysterious neighbors, of vanishing silently and leaving, if anything at all, corroding bits of metal out of which no one could make sense.

I had once stood in a graveyard that was a great fallen city. It was not hard to imagine another. After watching fruitlessly at intervals until winter was imminent, I promised myself a journey. After all, there was nothing to explain my disappointment. I had not known for what I was searching.

Or perhaps I did know, secretly, and would not admit it to myself: I wanted a miracle. Miracles, by definition, are without continuity, and perhaps my rooftop scientist had nudged me in that direction by the uncertainty of his departure. The only thing that characterizes a miracle, to my mind, is its sudden appearance and disappearance within the natural order, although, strangely, this loose definition would include each individual person. Miracles, in fact, momentarily dissolve the natural order or place themselves in opposition to it. My first experience had been only a tantalizing expectation, a hint that I must look elsewhere than in retorts or coiled wire, however formidable the powers that could be coerced to inhabit them. There was magic, but it was an autumnal, sad magic. I had a growing feeling that miracles were particularly concerned with life, with the animal aspect of things.

Just at this time, and with my thoughts in a receptive mood, a summons came that made it necessary for me to make a long night drive over poor roads through a dense forest. As a subjective experience, which it turned out to be, I would call it a near approach to what I was seeking. There was no doubt I was working further toward the heart of the problem. The common man thinks a miracle can just be "seen" to be reported. Quite the contrary. One has to be, I was discovering, reasonably sophisticated even to *perceive* the miraculous. It takes experience; otherwise, more miracles would be encountered.

One has, in short, to refine one's perceptions. Lightning bolts observed in attics, I now knew, were simply raw material, a lurking extravagant potential in the cosmos. In themselves, they were merely powers summoned up and released by the human mind. Wishing would never make them anything else and might make them worse. Nuclear fission was a ready example. No, a miracle was definitely something else, but that I would have to discover in my own good time.

Preoccupied with such thoughts, I started my journey of descent through the mountains. For a long time I was alone. I followed a road of unexpectedly twisting curves and abrupt descents. I bumped over ruts, where I occasionally caught the earthly starshine of eyes under leaves. Or I plunged at intervals into an impenetrable gloom buttressed by the trunks of huge pines.

After hours of arduous concentration and the sudden crimping of the wheel, my eyes were playing tricks with me. It was time to stop, but I could not afford to stop. I shook my head to clear it and blundered on. For a long time, in this confined glen among the mountains, I had been dimly aware that something beyond the reach of my headlights, but at times momentarily caught in their flicker, was accompanying me.

Whatever the creature might be, it was amazingly fleet. I never really saw its true outline. It seemed, at times, to my weary and much-rubbed eyes, to be running upright like a man, or, again, its color appeared to shift in a multiform illusion. Sometimes it seemed to be bounding forward. Sometimes it seemed to present a face to me and dance backward. From weary consciousness of an animal I grew slowly aware that the being caught momentarily in my flickering headlights was as much a shapeshifter as the wolf in a folk tale. It was not an animal; it was a gliding, leaping mythology. I felt the skin crawl on the back of my neck, for this was still the forest of the windigo and the floating heads commemorated so vividly in the masks of the Iroquois. I was lost, but I understood the forest. The blood that ran in me was not urban. I almost said not human. It had come from other times and a far place.

I slowed the car and silently fought to contain the horror that even animals feel before the disruption of the natural order. But was there a natural order? As I coaxed my lights to a fuller blaze I suddenly realized the absurdity of the question. Why should life tremble before the unexpected if it had not already anticipated the answer? There was no order. Or, better, what order there might be was far wilder and more formidable than that conjured up by human effort.

It did not help in the least to make out finally that the creature who had assigned himself to me was an absurdly spotted dog of dubious affinities—nor did it help that his coat had the curious properties generally attributable to a magician. For how, after all, could I assert with surety what shape this dog had originally possessed a half mile down the road? There was no way of securing his word for it.

The dog was, in actuality, an illusory succession of forms finally, but momentarily, frozen into the shape "dog" by me. A word, no more. But as it turned away into the night how was I to know it would remain "dog"? By experience? No, it had been picked by me out of a running weave of colors and faces into which it would lapse once more as it bounded silently into the inhuman, unpopulated wood. We deceive ourselves if we think our self-drawn categories exist there. The dog would simply become once more an endless running series of forms, which would not, the instant I might vanish, any longer know themselves as "dog."

By a mental effort peculiar to man, I had wrenched a leaping phantom into the flesh "dog," but the shape could not be held, neither his nor my own. We were contradictions and unreal. A nerve net and the lens of an eye had created us. Like the dog, I was destined to leap away at last into the unknown wood. My flesh, my own seemingly unique individuality, was already slipping like flying mist, like the colors of the dog, away from the little parcel of my bones. If there was order in us, it was the order of change. I started the car again, but I drove on chastened and unsure. Somewhere something was running and changing in the haunted wood. I knew no more than that. In a similar way, my mind was leaping and also changing as it sped. That was how the true miracle, my own miracle, came to me in its own time and fashion.

III

The episode occurred upon an unengaging and unfrequented shore. It began in the late afternoon of a day devoted at the start to ordinary scientific purposes. There was the broken prow of a beached boat subsiding in heavy sand, left by the whim of ancient currents a long way distant from the shifting coast. Somewhere on the horizon wavered the tenuous outlines of a misplaced building, growing increasingly insubstantial in the autumn light.

After my companions had taken their photographs and departed, their persistent voices were immediately seized upon and absorbed by the extending immensity of an incoming fog. The fog trailed in wisps over the upthrust ribs of the boat. For a time I could see it fingering the tracks of some small animal, as though engaged in a belated dialogue with the creature's mind. The tracks crisscrossed a dune, and there the fog hesitated, as though puzzled. Finally, it approached and enwrapped me, as though to peer into my face. I was not frightened, but I also realized with a slight shock that I was not intended immediately to leave.

I sat down then and rested with my back against the overturned boat. All around me the stillness intensified and the wandering tendrils of the fog continued their search. Nothing escaped them.

The broken cup of a wild bird's egg was touched tentatively, as if with meaning, for the first time. I saw a sand-colored ghost crab, hitherto hidden and immobile, begin to sidle amidst the beach grass as though imbued suddenly with a will derived ultimately from the fog. A gull passed high overhead, but its cry took on the plaint of something other than itself.

I began dimly to remember a primitive dialogue as to whether God is a mist or merely a mist maker. Since a great deal of my thought has been spent amidst such early human and, to my mind, not outworn speculations, the idea did not seem particularly irrational or blasphemous. How else would so great a being, assuming his existence, be able thoroughly to investigate his world, or, perhaps, merely a world that he had come upon, than as he was now proceeding to do?

I closed my eyes and let the tiny diffused droplets of the fog gently palpate my face. At the same time, by some unexplained affinity, I felt my mind drawn inland, to pour, smoking and gigantic as the fog itself, through the gorges of a neighboring mountain range.

In a little shaft of falling light my consciousness swirled dimly over the tombstones of a fallen cemetery. Something within me touched half-obliterated names and dates before sliding imperceptibly onward toward an errand in the city. That errand, whatever its purpose, perhaps because I was mercifully guided away from the future, was denied me.

As suddenly as I had been dispersed I found myself back among the boat timbers and the broken shell of something that had not achieved existence. "I am the thing that lives in the midst of the bones"—a line from the dead poet Charles Williams persisted obstinately in my head. It was true. I was merely condensed from that greater fog to a smaller congelation of droplets. Vague and smoky wisplets of thought were my extensions.

From a rack of bone no more substantial than the broken boat ribs on the beach, I was moving like that larger, all-investigating fog through the doorways of the past. Somewhere far away in an inland city the fog was transformed into a blizzard. Nineteen twenty-nine was a meaningless date that whipped by upon a flying newspaper. The blizzard was beating upon a great gate marked St. Elizabeth's. I was no longer the blizzard. I was hurrying, a small dark shadow, up a stairway beyond which came a labored and importunate breathing.

The man lay back among the pillows, wracked, yellow, and cadaverous. Though I was his son he knew me only as one lamp is briefly lit from another in the windy night. He was beyond speech, but a question was there, occupying the dying mind, excluding the living, something before which all remaining thought had to be mustered. At the time I was too young to understand. Only now could the hurrying shadow drawn from the wrecked boat interpret and relive the question. The starving figure on the bed was held back from death only by a magnificent heart that would not die.

I, the insubstantial substance of memory, the dispersed droplets of the ranging fog, saw the man lift his hands for the last time. Strangely, in all that ravished body, they alone had remained unchanged. They were strong hands, the hands of a craftsman who had played many roles in his life: actor, laborer, professional runner. They were the hands of a man, indirectly of all men, for such had been the nature of his life. Now, in a last lucid moment, he had lifted them up and, curiously, as though they belonged to another being, he had turned and flexed them, gazed upon them unbelievingly, and dropped them once more.

He, too, the shadow, the mist in the gaping bones, had seen these seemingly untouched deathless instruments rally as though with one last purpose before the demanding will. And I, also a shadow, come back across forty years, could hear the question at last. "Why are you, my hands, so separate from me at death, yet still to be commanded? Why have you served me, you who are alive and ingeniously clever?" For here he turned and contemplated them with his old superb steadiness. "What has been our partnership, for I, the shadow, am going, yet you of all of me are alive and persist?"

I could have sworn that his last thought was not of himself but of the fate of the instruments. He was outside, he was trying to look into the secret purposes of things, and the hands, the masterful hands, were the only purpose remaining, while he, increasingly without center, was vanishing. It was the hands that contained his last conscious act. They had been formidable in life. In death they had become strangers who had denied their master's last question.

Suddenly I was back under the overhang of the foundered boat. I had sat there stiff with cold for many hours. I was no longer the extension of a blizzard beating against immovable gates. The year of the locusts was done. It was, instead, the year of the mist maker that some obscure Macusi witch doctor had chosen to call god. But the mist maker had gone over the long-abandoned beach, touching for his inscrutable purposes only the broken shell of the nonexistent, only the tracks of a wayward fox, only a man who, serving the mist maker, could be made to stream wispily through the interstices of time.

I was a biologist, but I chose not to examine my hands. The fog and the night were lifting. I had been far away for hours. Crouched in my heavy sheepskin I waited without thought as the witch doctor might have waited for the morning dispersion of his god. Finally, the dawn began to touch the sea, and then the worn timbers of the hulk beside which I sheltered reddened just a little. It was then I began to glimpse the world from a different perspective.

I had watched for nights the great bolts leaping across the pane of an attic window, the bolts Emerson had dreamed in the first scientific days might be the force that hurled reptile into mammal. I had watched at midnight the mad scientists intent upon their own creation. But in the end, those fantastic flashes of the lightning had ceased without issue, at least for me. The pane, the inscrutable pane, had darkened at last; the scientists, if scientists they were, had departed, carrying their secret with them. I sighed, remembering. It was then I saw the miracle. I saw it because I was hunched at ground level, smelling rank of fox, and no longer gazing with upright human arrogance upon the things of this world.

I did not realize at first what it was that I looked upon. As my wandering attention centered, I saw nothing but two small projecting ears lit by the morning sun. Beneath them, a small neat face looked shyly up at me. The ears moved at every sound, drank in a gull's cry and the far horn of a ship. They crinkled, I began to realize, only with curiosity; they had not learned to fear. The creature was very young. He was alone in a dread universe. I crept on my knees around the prow and crouched beside him. It was a small fox pup from a den under the timbers who looked up at me. God knows what had become of his brothers and sisters. His parent must not have been home from hunting.

He innocently selected what I think was a chicken bone from an untidy pile of splintered rubbish and shook it at me invitingly. There was a vast and playful humor in his face. "If there was only one fox in the world and I could kill him, I would do." The words of a British poacher in a pub rasped in my ears. I dropped even further and painfully away from human stature. It has been said repeatedly that one can never, try as he will, get around to the front of the universe. Man is destined to see only its far side, to realize nature only in retreat.

Yet here was the thing in the midst of the bones, the wide-eyed, innocent fox inviting me to play, with the innate courtesy of its two forepaws placed appealingly together, along with a mock shake of the head. The universe was swinging in some fantastic fashion around to present its face, and the face was so small that the universe itself was laughing.

It was not a time for human dignity. It was a time only for the careful observance of amenities written behind the stars. Gravely I arranged my forepaws while the puppy whimpered with ill-concealed excitement. I drew the breath of a fox's den into my nostrils. On impulse, I picked up clumsily a whiter bone and shook it in teeth that had not entirely forgotten their original purpose. Round and round we tumbled for one ecstatic moment. We were the innocent thing in the midst of the bones, born in the egg, born in the den, born in the dark cave with the stone ax close to hand, born at last in human guise to grow coldly remote in the room with the rifle rack upon the wall.

But I had seen my miracle. I had seen the universe as it begins for all things. It was, in reality, a child's universe, a tiny and laughing universe. I rolled the pup on his back and ran, literally ran for the nearest ridge. The sun was half out of the sea, and the world was swinging back to normal. The adult foxes would be already trotting home.

A little farther on, I passed one on a ridge who knew well I had no gun, for it swung by quite close, stepping delicately with brush and head held high. Its face was watchful but averted. It did not matter. It was what I had experienced and the fox had experienced, what we had all experienced in adulthood. We passed carefully on our separate ways into the morning, eyes not meeting.

But to me the mist had come, and the mere chance of two lifted sunlit ears at morning. I knew at last why the man on the bed had smiled finally before he dropped his hands. He, too, had worked around to the front of things in his death agony. The hands were playthings and had to be cast aside at last like a little cherished toy. There was a meaning and there was not a meaning, and therein lay the agony.

The meaning was all in the beginning, as though time was awry. It was a little beautiful meaning that did not stay, and the sixty-year-old man on the hospital bed had traveled briefly toward it through the dark at the end of the universe. There was something in the desperate nature of the world that had to be reversed, but he had been too weak to tell me, and the hands had dropped helplessly away.

After forty years I had been just his own age when the fog had come groping for my face. I think I can safely put it down that I had been allowed my miracle. It was very small, as is the way of great things. I had been permitted to correct time's arrow for a space of perhaps five minutes—and that is a boon not granted to all men. If I were to render a report upon this episode, I would say that men must find a way to run the arrow backward. Doubtless it is impossible in the physical world, but in the memory and the will man might achieve the deed if he would try.

For just a moment I had held the universe at bay by the simple expedient of sitting on my haunches before a fox den and tumbling about with a chicken bone. It is the gravest, most meaningful act I shall ever accomplish, but, as Thoreau once remarked of some peculiar errand of his own, there is no use reporting it to the Royal Society.

The World Eaters

Really we create nothing.
We merely plagiarize nature.

JEAN BAITAILLON

It came to me in the night, in the midst of a bad dream, that perhaps man, like the blight descending on a fruit, is by nature a parasite, a spore bearer, a world eater. The slime molds are the only creatures on the planet that share the ways of man from his individual pioneer phase to his final immersion in great cities. Under the microscope one can see the mold amoebas streaming to their meeting places, and no one would call them human. Nevertheless, magnified many thousand times and observed from the air, their habits would appear close to our own. This is because, when their microscopic frontier is gone, as it quickly is, the single amoeboid frontiersmen swarm into concentrated aggregations. At the last they thrust up overtoppling spore palaces, like city skyscrapers. The rupture of these vesicles may disseminate the living spores as far away proportionately as man's journey to the moon.

It is conceivable that in principle man's motor throughways resemble the slime trails along which are drawn the gathering mucors that erect the spore palaces, that man's cities are only the ephemeral moment of his spawning— that he must descend upon the orchard of far worlds or die. Human beings are a strange variant in nature and a very recent one. Perhaps man has evolved as a creature whose centrifugal tendencies are intended to drive it as a blight is lifted and driven, outward across the night.

I do not believe, for reasons I will venture upon later, that this necessity is written in the genes of men, but it would be foolish not to consider the possibility, for man as an interplanetary spore bearer may be only at the first moment of maturation. After all, *Mucoroides* and its relatives must once have performed their act of dissemination for the very first time. In man, even if the feat is cultural, it is still possible that some incalculable and ancient urge lies hidden beneath the seeming rationality of institutionalized science. For example, a young space engineer once passionately exclaimed to me, "We must give all we have…" It was as though he were hypnotically compelled by that obscure chemical, acrasin, that draws the slime molds to their destiny. And is it not true also that observers like myself are occasionally bitterly castigated for daring to examine the motivation of our efforts toward space? In the intellectual climate of today one should strive to remember the words that Herman Melville accorded his proud, fate-confronting Captain Ahab, "All my means are sane, my motive and my object mad."

The cycles of parasites are often diabolically ingenious. It is to the unwilling host that their ends appear mad. Has earth hosted a new disease—that of the world eaters? Then inevitably the spores must fly. Short-lived as they are, they must fly. Somewhere far outward in the dark, instinct may intuitively inform them, lies the garden of the worlds. We must consider the possibility that we do not know the real nature of our kind. Perhaps *Homo sapiens,* the wise, is himself only a mechanism in a parasitic cycle, an instrument for the transference, ultimately, of a more invulnerable and heartless version of himself.

Or, again, the dark may bring him wisdom.

I stand in doubt as my forebears must once have done at the edge of the shrinking forest. I am a man of the rocket century; my knowledge, such as it is, concerns our past, our dubious present, and our possible future. I doubt our motives, but I grant us the benefit of the doubt and, like Arthur Clarke, call it, for want of a better term, "childhood's end." I also know, as did Plato, that one who has spent his life in the shadow of great wars may, like a captive, blink and be momentarily blinded when released into the light.

There are aspects of the world and its inhabitants that are eternal, like the ripples marked in stone on fossil beaches. There is a biological preordination that no one can change. These are seriatim events that only the complete reversal of time could undo. An example would be the moment when the bats dropped into the air and fluttered away from the insectivore line that gave rise to ourselves. What fragment of man, perhaps a useful fragment, departed with them? Something, shall we say, that had it lingered, might have made a small, brave, twilight difference in the mind of man.

There is a part of human destiny that is not fixed irrevocably but is subject to the flying shuttles of chance and will. Everyone imagines that he knows what is possible and what is impossible, but the whole of time and history attest our ignorance. One evening, in a drab and heartless area of the metropolis, a windborne milkweed seed circled my head. On impulse I seized the delicate aerial orphan which otherwise would have perished. Its long midwinter voyage seemed too favorable an augury to ignore. Placing the seed in my glove, I took it home into the suburbs and found a field in which to plant it. Of a million seeds blown on a vagrant wind into the city, it alone may survive.

Why did I bother? I suppose, in retrospect, for the sake of the future and the memory of the bats whirling like departing thoughts from the tree of ancestral man. Perhaps, after all, there lingered in my reflexes enough of a voyager to help all travelers on the great highway of the winds. Or perhaps I am not yet totally a planet eater and wished that something green might survive. A single impulse, a hand outstretched to an alighting seed, suggests that something is still undetermined in the human psyche, that the time trap has not yet closed inexorably. Some aspect of man that has come with him from the sunlit grasses is still instinctively alive and being fought for. The future, formidable as a thundercloud, is still inchoate and unfixed upon the horizon.

II

Man is "a tinkerer playing with ideas and mechanisms," comments a recent and very able writer upon technology, R. J. Forbes. He goes on to state that, if those impulses were to disappear, man would cease to be a human being in the sense we know. It is necessary to concede to Forbes that for Western man, *Homo faber,* the tool user, the definition is indeed appropriate. Nevertheless, when we turn to the people of the wilderness we must place certain limitations upon the words. That man has utilized tools through out his history is true, but that man has been particularly inventive or a tinkerer in the sense of seeking constant innovation is open to question.

Students of living primitives in backward areas such as Australia have found them addicted to immemorial usage in both ideas and tools. There is frequently a prejudice against the kind of change to which our own society has only recently adjusted. Such behavior is viewed askance as disruptive. The society is in marked ecological balance with its surroundings, and any drastic innovation from within the group is apt to be rejected as interfering with the will of the divine ancestors.

Not many years ago I fell to chatting with a naturalist who had had a long experience among the Cree of the northern forests. What had struck him about these Indians, even after considerable exposure to white men, was their remarkable and yet, in our terms, "indifferent" adjustment to their woodland environment. By indifference my informant meant that while totally skilled in the use of everything in their surroundings, they had little interest in experiment in a scientific sense, or in carrying objects about with them. Indeed they were frequently very careless with equipment or clothing given or loaned to them. Such things might be discarded after use or left hanging casually on a branch. One was left with the impression that these woodsmen were, by our standards, casual and feckless. Their reliance upon their own powers was great, but it was based on long traditional accommodation and a psychology by no means attuned to the civilized innovators' world. Plant fibers had their uses, wood had its uses, but everything from birch bark to porcupine quills was simply "given." Raw materials were always at hand, to be ignored or picked up as occasion demanded.

One carried little, one survived on little, and little in the way of an acquisitive society existed. One lived amidst all one had use for. If one shifted position in space the same materials were again present to be used. These people were ignorant of what Forbes would regard as the technological necessity to advance. Until the intrusion of whites, their technology had been long frozen upon a barely adequate subsistence level. "Progress" in Western terms was an unknown word.

Similarly I have heard the late Frank Speck discuss the failure of the Montagnais-Naskapi of the Labrador peninsula to take advantage, in their winter forest, either of Eskimo snow goggles, for which they substituted a mere sprig of balsam thrust under the cap, or of the snow house, which is far more comfortable than their cold and draft-exposed wigwams. The same indifference toward technological improvement or the acceptance of innovations from outside thus extended even to their racial brothers, the Eskimo. Man is a tool user, certainly, whether of the stone knife or less visible hunting magic. But that he is an obsessive innovator is far less clear. Tradition rules in the world's outlands. Man is not on this level driven to be inventive. Instead he is using the sum total of his environment almost as a single tool.

There is a very subtle point at issue here. H. C. Conklin, for example, writes about one Philippine people, the Hanunóo, that their "activities require an intimate familiarity with local plants.... Contrary to the assumption that subsistence level groups never use but a small segment of the local flora, ninety-three percent of the total number of native plant types are recognized ... as culturally significant." As Claude Lévi-Strauss has been at pains to point out, this state of affairs has been observed in many simple cultures.

Scores of terms exist for objects in the natural environment for which civilized man has no equivalents at all. The latter is engaged primarily with his deepening shell of technology which either exploits the natural world or thrusts it aside. By contrast, man in the earlier cultures was so oriented that the total natural environment occupied his exclusive attention. If parts of it did not really help him practically, they were often inserted into magical patterns that did. Thus man existed primarily in a carefully reorganized nature—one that was watched, brooded over, and managed by magico-religious as well as practical means.

Nature was actually as well read as an alphabet; it was the real "tool" by which man survived with a paucity of practical equipment. Or one could say that the tool had largely been forged in the human imagination. It consisted of the way man had come to organize and relate himself to the sum total of his environment. This world view was comparatively static. Nature was sacred and contained powers which demanded careful propitiation. Modern man, on the other hand, has come to look upon nature as a thing outside himself—an object to be manipulated or discarded at will. It is his technology and its vocabulary that makes his primary world. If, like the primitive, he has a sacred center, it is here. Whatever is potential must be unrolled, brought into being at any cost. No other course is conceived as possible. The economic system demands it.

Two ways of life are thus arrayed in final opposition. One way reads deep, if sometimes mistaken, analogies into nature and maintains toward change a reluctant conservatism. The other is fiercely analytical. Having consciously discovered sequence and novelty, man comes to transfer the operation of the world machine to human hands and to install change itself as progress. A reconciliation of the two views would seem to be necessary if humanity is to survive. The obstacles, however, are great.

Nowhere are they better illustrated than in the decades-old story of an anthropologist who sought to contact a wild and untouched group of aborigines in the red desert of central Australia. Traveling in a truck loaded with water and simple gifts, the scientist finally located his people some five hundred miles from the nearest white settlement. The anthropologist lived with the bush folk for a few weeks and won their confidence. They trusted him. The time came to leave. Straight over the desert ran the tracks of his car, and the aborigines are magnificent trackers.

Things were not the same when their friend had left; something had been transposed or altered in their landscape. The gifts had come so innocently. The little band set out one morning to follow the receding track of their friend. They were many days drifting on the march, drawn on perhaps by that dim impulse to which the slime molds yield. Eventually they came to the white man's frontier town. Their friend was gone, but there were other and less kindly white men. There were also drink, prostitution, and disease, about which they were destined to learn. They would never go back to the dunes and the secret places. In five years a begging and degraded remnant would stray through the outskirts of the settlers' town.

They had learned to their cost that it is possible to wander out of the world of the ancestors, only to become an object of scorn in a world directed to a different set of principles for which the aborigines had no guiding precedent. By leaving the timeless land they had descended into hell. Not all the tiny beings of the slime mold escape to new pastures; some wander, some are sacrificed to make the spore cities, and but a modicum of the original colony mounts the winds of space. It is so in the cities of men.

III

Over a century ago Samuel Taylor Coleridge ruminated in one of his own encounters with the universe that "A Fall of some sort or other— the creation as it were of the nonabsolute—is the fundamental postulate of the moral history of man. Without this hypothesis, man is unintelligible; with it every phenomenon is explicable. The mystery itself is too profound for human insight."

In making this observation Coleridge had come very close upon the flaw that was to create, out of a comparatively simple creature, the world eaters of the twentieth century. How, is a mystery to be explored, because every man on the planet belongs to the same species, and every man communicates. A span of three centuries has been enough to produce a planetary virus, while on that same planet a few lost tribesmen with brains the biological equal of our own peer in astonishment from the edges of the last wilderness.

One of the scholars of the scientific twilight, Joseph Glanvill, was quick to intimate that to posterity a voyage to the moon "will not be more strange than one to America." Even in 1665 the ambitions of the present century had entered human consciousness. The paradox is already present. There is the man *Homo sapiens* who in various obscure places around the world would rarely think of altering the simple tools of his forefathers, and, again, there is this same *Homo sapiens* in a wild flurry of modern thought patterns reversing everything by which he had previously lived. Such an episode parallels the rise of a biological mutation as potentially virulent in its effects as a new bacterial strain. The fact that its nature appears to be cultural merely enables the disease to be spread with fantastic rapidity. There is no comparable episode in history.

There are two things which are basic to an understanding of the way in which the primordial people differ from the world eaters, ourselves. Coleridge was quite right that man no more than any other living creature represented the absolute. He was finite and limited, and thus his ability to wreak his will upon the world was limited. He might dream of omniscient power, he might practice magic to obtain it, but such power remained beyond his grasp.

As a primitive, man could never do more than linger at the threshold of the energy that flickered in his campfire, nor could he hurl himself beyond Pluto's realm of frost. He was still within nature. True, he had restructured the green world in his mind so that it lay slightly ensorceled under the noonday sun. Nevertheless the lightning still roved and struck at will; the cobra could raise its deathly hood in the peasant's hut at midnight. The dark was thronged with spirits.

Man's powerful, undisciplined imagination had created a region beyond the visible spectrum which would sometimes aid and sometimes destroy him. Its propitiation and control would occupy and bemuse his mind for long millennia. To climb the fiery ladder that the spore bearers have used one must consume the resources of a world. Since such resources are not to be tapped without the drastic reordering of man's mental world, his final feat has as its first preliminary the invention of a way to pass knowledge through the doorway of the tomb—namely, the achievement of the written word.

Only so can knowledge be made sufficiently cumulative to challenge the stars. Our brothers of the forest have not lived in the world we have entered. They do not possess the tiny figures by which the dead can be made to speak from those great cemeteries of thought known as libraries. Man's first giant step for mankind was not through space. Instead it lay through time. Once more in the words of Glanvill, "That men should speak after their tongues were ashes, or communicate with each other in differing Hemisphears, before the Invention of Letters could not but have been thought a fiction."

In the first of the world's cities man had begun to live against the enormous backdrop of the theatre. He had become self-conscious, a man enacting his destiny before posterity. As ruler, conqueror, or thinker he lived, as Lewis Mumford has put it, by and for the record. In such a life both evil and good come to cast long shadows into the future. Evil leads to evil, good to good, but frequently the former is the most easy for the cruel to emulate. Moreover, when invention lends itself to centralized control, the individualism of the early frontiers easily gives way to routinized conformity. If life is made easier it is also made more dependent. If artificial demands are stimulated, resources must be consumed at an ever-increasing pace.

As in the microscopic instance of the slime molds, the movement into the urban aggregations is intensified. The most technically advanced peoples will naturally consume the lion's share of the earth's resources. Thus the United States at present, representing some six percent of the world's population, consumes over thirty-four percent of its energy and twenty-nine percent of its steel. Over a billion pounds of trash are spewed over the landscape in a single year. In these few elementary facts, which are capable of endless multiplication, one can see the shape of the future growing—the future of a planet virus *Homo sapiens* as he assumes in his technological phase what threatens to be his final role.

Experts have been at pains to point out that the accessible crust of the earth is finite, while the demand for minerals steadily increases as more and more societies seek for themselves a higher, Westernized standard of living. Unfortunately many of these sought-after minerals are not renewable, yet a viable industrial economy demands their steady output. A rising world population requiring an improved standard of living clashes with the oncoming realities of a planet of impoverished resources.

"We live in an epoch of localized affluence," asserts Thomas Levering, an expert on mineral resources. A few shifts and subterfuges may, with increasing effort and expense, prolong this affluence, but no feat of scientific legerdemain can prevent the eventual exhaustion of the world's mineral resources at a time not very distant. It is thus apparent that to apply to Western industrial man the term "world eater" is to do so neither in derision nor contempt. We are facing, instead, a simple reality to which, up until recently, the only response has been flight— the flight outward from what appears unsolvable and which threatens, in the end, to leave an impoverished human remnant clinging to an equally impoverished globe.

So quick and so insidious has been the rise of the world virus that its impact is just beginning to be felt and its history to be studied. Basically man's planetary virulence can be ascribed to just one thing: a rapid ascent, particularly in the last three centuries, of an energy ladder so great that the line on the chart representing it would be almost vertical. The event, in the beginning, involved only Western European civilization. Today it increasingly characterizes most of the planet.

The earliest phase of the human acquisition of energy beyond the needs of survival revolves, as observed earlier, around the rise of the first agricultural civilizations shortly after the close of the Ice Age. Only with the appearance of wealth in the shape of storable grains can the differentiation of labor and of social classes, as well as an increase in population, lay the basis for the expansion of the urban world. With this event the expansion of trade and trade routes was sure to follow. The domestication of plants and animals, however, was still an event of the green world and the sheepfold. Nevertheless it opened a doorway in nature that had lain concealed from man.

Like all earth's other creatures, he had previously existed in a precarious balance with nature. In spite of his adaptability, man, the hunter, had spread across the continents like thin fire burning over a meadow. It was impossible for his numbers to grow in any one place, because man, multiplying, quickly consumes the wild things upon which he feeds and then himself faces starvation. Only with plant domestication is the storage granary made possible and through it three primary changes in the life of man: a spectacular increase in human numbers; diversification of labor; the ability to feed from the countryside the spore cities into which man would presently stream.

After some four million years of lingering in nature's shadow, man would appear to have initiated a drastic change in the world of the animal gods and the magic that had seen him through millennial seasons. Such a change did not happen overnight, and we may never learn the details of its incipient beginnings. As we have already noted, at the close of the Ice Age, and particularly throughout the northern hemisphere, the big game, the hairy mammoth and mastodon, the giant long-horned bison, had streamed away with the melting glaciers. Sand was blowing over the fertile plains of North Africa and the Middle East. Gloomy forests were springing up in the Europe of the tundra hunters. The reindeer and musk ox had withdrawn far into the north on the heels of the retreating ice.

Man must have turned, in something approaching agony and humiliation, to the women with their digging sticks and arcane knowledge of seeds. Slowly, with greater ceremonial, the spring and harvest festivals began to replace the memory of the "gods with the wet nose," the bison gods of the earlier free-roving years. Whether for good or ill the world would never be the same. The stars would no longer be the stars of the wandering hunters. Halley's comet returning would no longer gleam on the tossing antlers and snowy backs of the moving game herds. Instead it would glimmer from the desolate tarns left by the ice in dark forests or startle shepherds watching flocks on the stony hills of Judea. Perhaps it was the fleeting star seen by the three wise men of legend, for a time of human transcendence was approaching.

To comprehend the rise of the world eaters one must leap centuries and millennia. To account for the rise of high-energy civilization is as difficult as to explain the circumstances that have gone into the creation of man himself. Certainly the old sun-plant civilizations provided leisure for meditation, mathematics, and transport energy through the use of sails. Writing, which arose among them, created a kind of stored thought-energy, an enhanced social brain.

All this the seed-and-sun world contributed, but no more. Not all of these civilizations left the traditional religious round of the seasons or the worship of the sun-kings installed on earth. Only far on in time, in west Europe, did a new culture and a new world emerge. Perhaps it would be best to limit our exposition to one spokesman who immediately anticipated its appearance. "If we must select some one philosopher as the hero of the revolution in scientific method," maintained William Whewell, the nineteenth-century historian, "beyond all doubt Francis Bacon occupies the place of honor." This view is based upon four simple precepts, the first of which, from *The Advancement of Learning,* I will give in Bacon's own words. "As the foundation," he wrote, "we are not to imagine or suppose, but to *discover* what nature does or may be made to do." Today this sounds like a truism. In Bacon's time it was a novel, analytical, and unheard-of way to explore nature. Bacon was thus the herald of what has been called "the invention of inventions"—the scientific method itself.

He believed also that the thinker could join with the skilled worker—what we today would call the technologist—to conduct experiment more ably than by simple and untested meditation in the cloister. Bacon, in other words, was groping toward the idea of the laboratory, of a whole new way of schooling. Within such schools, aided by government support, he hoped for the solution of problems not to be dealt with "in the hourglass of one man's life." In expressing this hope he had recognized that great achievement in science must not wait on the unaided and rare genius, but that research should be institutionalized and supported over the human generations.

Fourth and last of Bacon's insights was his vision of the future to be created by science. Here there clearly emerges that orientation toward the future which has since preoccupied the world of science and the West. Bacon was preeminently the spokesman of *anticipatory* man. The long reign of the custom-bound scholastics was at an end. Anticipatory analytical man, enraptured by novelty, was about to walk an increasingly dangerous pathway.

He would triumph over disease and his numbers would mount; steam and, later, air transport would link the ends of the earth. Agriculture would fall under scientific management, and fewer men on the land would easily support the febrile millions in the gathering cities. As Glanvill had foreseen, thought would fly upon the air. Man's telescopic eye would rove through the galaxy and beyond. No longer would men be burned or tortured for dreaming of life on far-off worlds.

There came, too, in the twentieth century to mock the dream of progress the most ruthless and cruel wars of history. They were the first wars fought with total scientific detachment. Cities were firebombed, submarines turned the night waters into a flaming horror, the air was black with opposing air fleets.

The laboratories of Bacon's vision produced the atom bomb and toyed prospectively with deadly nerve gas. "Overkill" became a professional word. Iron, steel, Plexiglas, and the deadly mathematics of missile and anti-missile occupied the finest constructive minds. Even before space was entered, man began to assume the fixed mask of the robot. His courage was unbreakable, but in society there was mounting evidence of strain. Billions of dollars were being devoured in the space effort, while at the same time an affluent civilization was consuming its resources at an ever-increasing rate. Air and water and the land itself were being polluted by the activities of a creature grown used to the careless ravage of a continent.

Francis Bacon had spoken one further word on the subject of science, but by the time that science came its prophet had been forgotten.

He had spoken of learning as intended to bring an enlightened life. Western man's ethic is not directed toward the preservation of the earth that fathered him. A devouring frenzy is mounting as his numbers mount. It is like the final movement in the spore palaces of the slime molds. Man is now only a creature of anticipation feeding upon events.

"When evil comes it is because two gods have disagreed," runs the proverb of an elder people. Perhaps it is another way of saying that the past and the future are at war in the heart of man. On March 7, 1970, as I sit at my desk the eastern seaboard is swept by the shadow of the greatest eclipse since 1900. Beyond my window I can see a strangely darkened sky, as though the light of the sun were going out forever. For an instant, lost in the dim gray light, I experience an equally gray clarity of vision.

IV

There is a tradition among the little Bushmen of the Kalahari desert that eclipses of the moon are caused by Kingsfoot, the lion who covers the moon's face with his paw to make the night dark for hunting. Since our most modern science informs us we have come from animals, and since almost all primitives have tended to draw their creator gods from the animal world with which they were familiar, modern man and his bush contemporaries have arrived at the same conclusion by very different routes. Both know that they are shape shifters and changelings. They know their relationship to animals by different ways of logic and different measures of time.

Modern man, the world eater, respects no space and no thing green or furred as sacred. The march of the machines has entered his blood. They are his seed boxes, his potential wings and guidance systems on the far roads of the universe. The fruition time of the planet virus is at hand. It is high autumn, the autumn before winter topples the spore cities. "The living memory of the city disappears," writes Mumford of this phase of urban life; "its inhabitants live in a self-annihilating moment to moment continuum." The ancestral center exists no longer. Anonymous millions roam the streets.

On the African veldt the lion, the last of the great carnivores, is addressed by the Bushmen over a kill whose ownership is contested. They speak softly the age-old ritual words for the occasion, "Great Lions, Old Lions, we know that you are brave." Nevertheless the little, almost weaponless people steadily advance. The beginning and the end are dying in unison and the one is braver than the other. Dreaming on by the eclipse-darkened window, I know with a sudden sure premonition that Kingsfoot has put his paw once more against the moon. The animal gods will come out for one last hunt.

Beginning on some winter night the snow will fall steadily for a thousand years and hush in its falling the spore cities whose seed has flown. The delicate traceries of the frost will slowly dim the glass in the observatories and all will be as it had been before the virus wakened. The long trail of Halley's comet, once more returning, will pass like a ghostly match flame over the unwatched grave of the cities. This has always been their end, whether in the snow or in the sand.

The Spore Bearers

*Either the machine has a meaning to life that we have not
yet been able to interpret in a rational manner, or it is itself
a manifestation of life and therefore mysterious.*

GARET GARRETT

It is a remarkable fact that much of what man has achieved through
the use of his intellect, nature had invented before him. *Pilobolus*, another fungus which prepares, sights, and fires its spore capsule, constitutes a curious anticipation of human rocketry. The fungus is one
that grows upon the dung of cattle. To fulfill its life cycle, its spores
must be driven up and outward to land upon vegetation several feet
away, where they may be eaten by grazing cows or horses.

The spore tower that discharges the *Pilobolus* missile is one of the
most fascinating objects in nature. A swollen cell beneath the black
capsule that contains the spores is a genuinely light-sensitive "eye."
This pigmented eye controls the direction of growth of the spore can-
non and aims it very carefully at the region of the greatest light in
order that no intervening obstacle may block the flight of the spore
capsule.

When a pressure of several atmospheres has been built up chemi-
cally within the cell underlying the spore container, the cell explodes,
blasting the capsule several feet into the air. Since firing takes place in

the morning hours, the stalks point to the sun at an angle sure to carry the tiny "rocket" several feet away as well as up. Tests in which the light has been reduced to a small spot indicate that the firing eye aims with remarkable accuracy. The spore vessel itself is so equipped with a quick-drying glue as to adhere to vegetation always in the proper position. Rain will not wash it off, and there it waits an opportunity to be taken up by munching cattle in order that *Pilobolus* can continue its travels through the digestive tract of the herbivores.

The tiny black capsule that bears the living spores through space is strangely reminiscent, in miniature, of man's latest adventure. Man, too, is a spore bearer. The labor of millions and the consumption of vast stores of energy are necessary to hurl just a few individuals, perhaps eventually people of both sexes, on the road toward another planet. Similarly, for every spore city that arises in the fungus world, only a few survivors find their way into the future.

It is useless to talk of transporting the excess population of our planet elsewhere, even if a world of sparkling water and green trees were available. In nature it is a law that the spore cities die, but the spores fly on to find their destiny. Perhaps this will prove to be the rule of the newborn planet virus. Somehow in the *mysterium* behind genetics, the tiny pigmented eye and the rocket capsule were evolved together.

In an equal mystery that we only pretend to understand, man, in the words of Garet Garrett, "reached with his mind into emptiness and seized the machine." Deathly though some of its effects have proved, robber of the earth's crust though it may appear at this human stage to be, perhaps there are written within the machine two ultimate possibilities. The first, already, if primitively, demonstrated, is that of being a genuine spore bearer of the first complex organism to cross the barrier of the void. The second is that of providing the means by which man may someday be able to program his personality, or its better aspects, into the deathless machine itself, and thus escape, or nearly escape, the mortality of the body.

This may well prove to be an illusory experiment, but we who stand so close under the green primeval shade may still be as incapable of evaluating the human future as the first ape-man would have been to chart the course of *Homo sapiens*. There are over one hundred thousand spores packed in a single capsule of *Pilobolus*, and but few such capsules will ever reach their destiny. This is the way of spore cities, in the infinite prodigality of nature. It may well be the dictum that controls the fate of man. Perhaps Rome drove blindly toward it and failed in the marches of the West. In the dreaming Buddhist cities that slowly ebbed away beneath the jungle, something was said that lingers not entirely forgotten—namely, "Thou canst not travel on the Path before thou hast become the Path itself." Perhaps written deep in ourselves is a simulacrum of the Way and the mind's deep spaces to travel. If so, our goal is light-years distant, even though year by year the gantries lengthen over the giant rockets.

Man possesses the potential power to reach all the planets in this system. None, so far as can be presently determined, offers the prospects of extended colonization. The journey, however, will be undertaken as President Nixon has announced. It will be pursued because the technological and psychological commitment to space is too great for Western culture to abandon. In spite of the breadth of the universe we have previously surveyed, a nagging hope persists that someday, by means unavailable at present, we might achieve the creation of a rocket ship operating near the speed of light. At this point we would enter upon unknown territory, for it has been argued on the basis of relativity theory that men in such a mechanism might exist on a different time scale and age less rapidly than man upon earth. Assuming that such were the case, question arises whether such a ship, coasting around the galaxy or beyond, might return to find life on our planet long departed. The disparities and the problems are great, and the conflicts of authorities have not made them less so.

It has been pointed out that so great a physicist as Sir Ernest Rutherford, as late as 1936, had pronounced the use of nuclear energy to be Utopian, at least within this century. Similar speculations on the part of others suggest that a great scientist's attempts to extrapolate his knowledge into the future may occasionally prove as inaccurate as the guesses of laymen. Scientific training is apt to produce a restraint, laudable enough in itself, that can readily degenerate into a kind of institutional conservatism. Darwin saw and commented upon this in his time. History has a way of outguessing all of us, but she does it in retrospect.

Nevertheless, because man is small and growing ever lonelier in his expanding universe, there remains a question he is unlikely ever to be able to answer. It involves the discovery of other civilizations in the cosmos. In some three billion years of life on this planet, man, who occupies a very small part of the geological time scale, is the one creature of earth who has achieved the ability to reason on a high abstract level. He has only grasped the nature of the stars within the last few generations. The number of such stars in the universe cannot be counted. Some may possess planets. Judging by our own solar system, of those planets few will possess life. Fewer still, infinitely fewer, will possess what could be called "civilizations" developed by other rational creatures.

On the basis of pure statistical chance, the likelihood that such civilizations are located in our portion of the galaxy is very small. Man's end may well come upon him long before he has had time to locate or even to establish the presence of other intelligent creatures in the universe. There are far more stars in the heavens than there are men upon the earth. The waste to be searched is too great for the powers we possess. In gambling terms, the percentage lies all with the house, or rather with the universe. Lonely though we may feel ourselves to be, we must steel ourselves to the fact that man, even far future man, may pass from the scene without possessing either negative or positive evidence of the existence of other civilized beings in this or other galaxies.

This is said with all due allowance for the fact that we may learn to make at least some satellites or planets within our own solar system artificially capable, in a small way, of sustaining life. For man to spread widely on the dubious and desert worlds of this sun system is unlikely. Much more unlikely is the chance that coursing at near the speed of light over a single arm of this galaxy would ever reveal intelligence, even if it were there. The speed would be too high and the planetary body too small. The size of our near neighbors, Mars and Venus, is proportionately tiny beside the sun's diameter or even that of the huge outer planets Jupiter and Saturn.

I have suggested that man-machines and finally pure intelligent machines—the product of a biology and a computerized machine technology beyond anything this century will possess—might be launched by man and dispersed as his final spore flight through the galaxies. Such machines would not need to trouble themselves with the time problem and, as the capsules of *Pilobolus* carry spores, might even be able to carry refrigerated human egg cells held in suspended animation and prepared to be activated, educated, and to grow up alone under the care of the machines.

The idea is fantastically wasteful, but so is life. It would be sufficient if the proper planetary conditions were discovered once in a thousand times. These human-machine combinations are much spoken of nowadays under the term "cyborg"—a shorthand term for "cybernetic organism." The machine structures would be intimately controlled by the human brain but built in such a manner as to amplify and extend the powers of the human personality. Other machines might be controlled by human beings deliberately modified by man's increasing knowledge of micro-surgery and genetics. Science has speculated that man has reached an evolutionary plateau. To advance beyond that plateau he must either intimately associate himself with machines in a new way or give way to "exosomatic evolution" and, in some fashion, transfer himself and his personality to the machine.

These are matters of the shadowy future and must be considered only as remote possibilities. More likely is the stricture that, even if we do not destroy ourselves as a planet virus, we will exhaust the primary resources of earth before we can produce the kind of spore carriers of which we dream. Again, the conception may lie forever beyond us. There is a certain grandeur, however, in thought of man in some far future hour battling against oblivion by launching a final spore flight of cyborgs through the galaxy—a haven-seeking flight projected by those doomed never to know its success or failure, a flight such as life itself has always engaged in since it arose from the primeval waters.

One must repeat that nature is extravagant in the expenditure of individuals and germ cells. Our remote half-human ancestors gave themselves and never expected, or got, an answer as to the destiny their descendants might serve or if, indeed, they would survive. This is still the road we tread in the twentieth century. Sight of the future is denied us, and life was never given to be bearable. To what far creature, whether of metal or of flesh, we may be the bridge, no word informs us. If such a being is destined to come, there can be no assurance that it will spare a thought for the men who, in the human dawn, prepared its way. Man is a part of that torrential living river, which, since the beginning, has instinctively known the value of dispersion. He will yearn therefore to spread beyond the planet he now threatens to devour. This thought persists and is growing. It is rooted in the psychology of man.

A story has been told of the founder of one of the world's great religions—a religion which seeks constantly, in its higher manifestations, to wipe clean the mirror of the mind. Buddha is reported to have said to his sorrowing disciples as he lay dying, "Walk on." He wanted his people to be free of earthly entanglement or desire. That is how one should go in dignity to the true harvest of the worlds. It is a philosophy transferred from the old sun civilizations of earth. It implies that one cannot proceed upon the path of human transcendence until one has made interiorly in one's soul a road into the future. This is the warning of one who knew that the spaces within stretch as far as those without. Cyborgs and exosomatic evolution, however far they are carried, partake of the planet virus. They will never bring peace to man, but they will harry him onward through the circle of the worlds.

II

A scientific civilization in the full sense is an anomaly in world history. The civilizations of the sun never developed it. Only one culture, that of the West, has, through technology, reduced the religious mystique so long attached to agriculture. Never before have such large masses of people been so totally divorced from the land or the direct processing of their own foodstuffs.

This phenomenon has undoubtedly contributed to the alienation of man from nature, as more and more acres go under cement for parking lots, shopping centers, and superhighways. A steadily mounting population threatens increasing damage to the natural environment from which food and breathable air are drawn. All kinds of sidelong, not very visible or dramatic dangers lurk about the edges of such an unstable situation. Any one of them could at some point become lethal, and an obscure and ignored problem turn into a disaster.

The tragedy of a single man in the New York blackout in 1965 could easily become the symbol for an entire civilization. This man, as it happened, was trapped by the darkness on an upper floor of a skyscraper. A Negrito or any one of the bush folk would have known better than to go prowling in a spirit-haunted, leopard-infested jungle after nightfall. The forest dwellers would have remained in their huts until daybreak.

In this case civilized man was troubled by no such inhibitions. Seizing a candle from a desk in his office, he made his way out into the corridor. Since the elevators were not running, he cast about for a stairway. Sighting what in the candlelight appeared to be a small service doorway near the bank of elevators, he opened it and, holding his small candle at eye level, stepped in. He was found the next day at the bottom of the elevator shaft, the extinguished candle still clutched in his hand.

I have said that this episode is symbolic. Man, frail, anticipatory man, no longer possessed the caution to find his way through a disturbance in his nightly routine. Instead he had seized a candle, the little flickering light of human knowledge, with which to confront one of his own giant creations in the dark. A janitor had left a door unlocked that should have been secured. Urban man, used to walking on smooth surfaces, had never glanced below his feet. He and his inadequate candle had plunged recklessly forward and been swallowed up as neatly by a machine in its tunnel as by a leopard on a dark path.

I have seen similar errors made at the onset of floods by men who no longer had the wit or conditioning to harken to the whispered warnings of wild nature. They had grown too confident of the powers of their own world, from which nature , so they thought, had been excluded. In the wider context of civilization, our candle flame may illuminate the next few moments but scarcely more. The old precarious world from which we came lurks always behind the door. It will find a way to be present, even if we should force it to retreat to the nearest star. Moreover, if, after the crust of the earth has been rifled and its resources consumed, civilization were to come upon evil times, man would have to start over with incredibly less than lay potentially before the flint users of the Ice Age.

But there emerges to haunt us the question of why this peculiar civilization arose. In the first part of the twentieth century appeared a man destined to be widely read, criticized, and contended against, even to be called wicked. He was destined to influence the philosophical historians who followed him in the attempt to observe some kind of discernible pattern in the events of history. Our concern with this man, Oswald Spengler, and his book, *The Decline of the West*, relates to just one aspect of Spengler's thought: the rise of our scientific civilization. That Spengler is periodically declared outmoded or resurrected need not involve us. What does affect us is that the man is basically a German poet-philosopher who glimpsed the leitmotif of the era we have been discussing and who pictured it well. It is the world in which we of the West find ourselves. Spengler is difficult, but in this aspect of his work he pictures the idea forms, the *zeitgeist,* lurking within the culture from which the rocket was to emerge.

Perhaps what he terms the Faustian culture—our own—began as early as the eleventh century with the growing addiction to great unfillable cathedrals with huge naves and misty recesses where space seemed to hover without limits. In the words of one architect, the Gothic arch is "a bow always tending to expand." Hidden within its tensions is the upward surge of the space rocket.

Again, infinite solitude tormented the individual soul. A too guilty hunger for forbidden knowledge beset the introverted heroes of this culture. The legend of Faust to this day epitomizes the West; the Quest of the Holy Grail is another of its Christian symbols. The bell towers of Western Europe have rung of time and death and burial in a way characteristic of no other culture. The bells were hung high and intended to reach far across space.

Faustian man is never at rest in the world. He is never the contemplative beneath the sacred Bô tree of the Buddha. He is, instead, a spokesman of the will. He is the embodiment of a restless, exploratory, and anticipating ego. In that last word we have the human head spun round to confront its future—the future it has created. It well may be that the new world, which began amidst timetolling bells and the stained glass and dim interiors of Gothic cathedrals, laid an enchantment upon the people of Western Europe that provided at least a portion of the seedbed for the later rise of science—just as guilt has also haunted us. In its highest moments, science could also be said, not irreverently, to be a search for the Holy Grail. There the analogy lies—a poet's vision perhaps, but a powerful one. I would merely add one observation: that the owl, Minerva's symbol of wisdom, is able to turn its head through an angle of one hundred and sixty degrees. It can be not visually anticipatory alone, it can look backward. Perhaps it is the lack of this ability that gives modern man and his children a slightly inhuman cast of countenance.

III

Giordano Bruno was burned at Rome in 1600. His body perished, but the ideas for which he died—the heretical concepts of the great depths of the universe and of life on other worlds—ran on with similar dreams across the centuries to enlighten our own time. Space travel unconsciously began when the first hunters took their bearings on the North Star or saw the rising of the Southern Cross. It grew incipiently with the mathematics and the magnetic needle of the mariners. Man, in retrospect, seems almost predestined for space. To master the dream in its entirety, however, man had to invent in two categories: inventions of power and inventions of understanding. The invention of the scientific method itself began as an adventure in understanding. Inventions of power without understanding have been the bane of human history.

The word "invention" can denote ideas far removed from the machines to which the people of our mechanically inclined era seek constantly to limit the word. Let us take one refined example. The zero, invented twice in the mists of prehistory, once by the Hindus and once by the Maya, lies at the root of all complicated mathematics, yet it is not a "thing." Rather, it is a "no thing," a "nothing," without which Roman mathematics was a heavy, lumbering affair. In our time that necessary zero leaps instantaneously through the circuits of computers, helping to guide a rocket on the long pathway to Mars. One might say that an unknown mathematical genius seeking pure abstract understanding was a necessary prehistoric prelude to the success of the computer. He was also, and tragically, the possible indirect creator of world disaster in the shape of atomic war.

"Traveling long journeys is costly, at all times troublesome, at some times dangerous," warned a seventeenth-century writer. These were true words spoken of great seas and unmapped continents. They can also be spoken of the scientific journey itself. Today, magnified beyond the comprehension of that ancient wayfarer, we contemplate roads across the planetary orbits, the penetration of unknown atmospheres, and the defiance of solar flares. This effort has become the primary obsession of the great continental powers. Into the organization of this endeavor has gone an outpouring of wealth and inventive genius so vast that it constitutes a public sacrifice equivalent in terms of relative wealth to the building of the Great Pyramid at Giza almost five thousand years ago. Indeed, there is a sense in which modern science is involved in the construction of just such a pyramid, though an invisible one.

Science, too, demands great sacrifice, persistence of purpose across the generations, and an almost religious devotion. Whether its creations will loom to future ages as strangely antiquated as the sepulchres of the divine pharaohs, time alone will tell. Perhaps, in the final reckoning, only understanding will enable man to look back upon his pathway. For if inventions of power outrun understanding, as they now threaten to do, man may well sink into a night more abysmal than any he has yet experienced. Understanding increasingly begets power, but, as perceptive statesmen have long observed, power in the wrong hands has a way of corrupting understanding.

There is an eye atop Palomar Mountain that peers at fleeing galaxies so remote that eons have elapsed since the light which reaches that great lens began its journey. There is another eye, that of the electron microscope, which peers deep into our own being. Both eyes are important. They are eyes of understanding. They balance and steady each other. They give our world perspective; they place man where he belongs. Such eyes, however, are subject to their human makers. Men may devise or acquire, and use beautiful or deathly machines and yet have no true time sense, no tolerance, no genuine awareness of their own history. By contrast, the balanced eye, the rare true eye of understanding, can explore the gulfs of history in a night or sense with uncanny accuracy the subtle moment when a civilization in all its panoply of power turns deathward. There are such troubled seers among us today—men who fear that the ramifications of the huge industrial complex centering upon space is draining us of energy and wealth for other enterprises—that it has about it a threatening, insensitive, and cataclysmic quality.

A term in military parlance, "the objective," may be pertinent here. It is intended to secure the mind against the diffuse and sometimes inept opportunism of the politician, or the waves of uninformed emotion to which the general public is so frequently subjected. An objective is delimited with precision and care. Its intention is to set a clearly defined goal. Armies, or for that matter sciences, do not advance on tides of words. Instead, they must be supplied logistically. Schedules must equate with a realistic appraisal of resources.

There will never be enough men or material for a multitudinous advance on all fronts—even for a wealthy nation. Thus, as our technological feats grow more costly, the objectives of our society must be assessed with care. From conservation to hospitals, from defense to space, we are forced by circumstance to live more constantly in the future. Random "tinkering," random response to the unexpected, become extraordinarily costly in the industrial world which Western society has created. Yet, paradoxically, the unexpected comes with increasing rapidity upon future-oriented societies such as ours. Psychological stresses appear. The current generation feels increasingly alienated from its predecessors. There is a quickening of vibrations running throughout the society. One might, in physiological terms, say that its metabolism has been feverishly accelerated. For this, a certain price in stability has been exacted, the effects of which may not be apparent until long afterward.

The attempt to conquer space has seized the public imagination. To many of this generation, the sight of rockets roaring upward has brought home the feats of science so spectacularly that we sometimes forget the medical researcher brooding in his laboratory, or the archaeologist striving amidst broken shards and undeciphered hieroglyphs to understand what doom destroyed a city lying beneath the sands of centuries. The estimated cost of placing the unmanned Surveyor 3 upon the moon amounted to more than eighty million dollars. Just one unmanned space probe, in other words, equaled or exceeded the entire endowment of many a good college or university; the manned flight of Apollo 12 cost two hundred and fifty millions. The total space program is inconceivably costly, yet the taxpayer, up until recently, accepted it with little question. By contrast, his elected officials frequently boggle over the trifling sums necessary to save a redwood forest or to clear a river of pollution.

What then, we are forced to ask, is our objective? Is it scientific? Is it purely military? Or is it these and more? Is there some unconscious symbolism at work? At heart, does each one of us, when a rocket hurtles into space, yearn once more for some lost green continent under other skies? Is humanity, like some ripening giant puffball, feeling the mounting pressure of the spores within? Are we, remote though we may be from habitable planets, driven by the same irresistible migrating impulse that descends upon an overpopulated hive? Are we each unconsciously escaping from the mechanized routine and urban troubles which increasingly surround us? Beneath our conscious rationalizations does this play a role in our willingness to sustain the growing burden?

Any answers to these questions would be complex and would vary from individual to individual. They are worth asking because they are part of the venture in understanding that is necessary to human survival. Two successful moon landings, it goes without saying, are an enormous intellectual achievement. But what we must try to understand is more difficult than mathematics of a moon shot—namely, the nature of the scientific civilization we are in the process of creating. Science has risen in a very brief interval into a giant social institution of enormous prestige and governmentally supported power. To many, it replaces primitive magic as the solution for all human problems.

IV

In the coastal jungles of eastern Mexico the archaeologist comes at intervals upon giant stone heads of many tons weight carved in a strikingly distinct style far different from that of the Maya. They mark the remains of the lost Olmec culture of the first millennium before the Christian era. Around the globe, more than one such society of clever artisans has arisen and placed its stamp, the order of its style, upon surrounding objects, only to lapse again into the night of time. Each was self-contained. Each, with the limited amount of wealth and energy at its disposal, placed its greatest emphasis upon some human dream, some lost philosophy, some inner drive beyond the satisfaction of the needs of the body. Each, in turn, vanished.

Western man, with the triumph of the experimental method, has turned upon the world about him an intellectual instrument of enormous power never fully exploited by any previous society. Its feats of understanding include the discovery of evolutionary change as revealed in the stratified rocks. It has looked far down the scale of life to reveal man magically shrunken to a tiny tree shrew on a forest branch. Science has solved the mysteries of microbial disease and through the spectroscope has determined the chemical composition of distant stars. It has groped its way into a knowledge of the gigantic distances of the cosmos—distances too remote for short-lived man ever to penetrate. It has learned why the sun endures and at what pace light leaps across the universe.

Man can speak into infinite spaces, but in this time in which I write violence and contention rage, not alone on opposite sides of the world, but here at home. How far are all these voices traveling, I wonder? Out beyond earth's farthest shadow, on and on into the depths of the universe? And suppose that there were, out yonder, some hidden listening ear, would it be able to discern any difference between the sounds man made when he was a chittering tree shrew contesting for a beetle and those produced at his appearance before a parliament of nations?

It is a thing to consider, because with understanding arise instruments of power, which always spread faster than the inventions of calm understanding. The tools of violence appeal to the fanatic, the illiterate, the blindly venomous. The inventions of power have grown monstrous in our time. Man's newfound ingenuity has given him health, wealth, and increase, but there is added now the ingredient of an ever-growing terror. Man is only beginning dimly to discern that the ultimate menace, the final interior zero, may lie in his own nature. It is said in an old tale that to understand life man must learn to shudder. This century seems doomed to master the lesson.

Science, in spite of its awe-inspiring magnitude, contains one flaw that partakes of the nature of the universe itself. It can solve problems, but it also creates them in a genuinely confusing ratio. They escape unseen out of the laboratory into the body politic, whether they be germs inured to antibiotics, the waiting death in rocket silos, or the unloosed multiplying power of life. There are just so many masterful and inventive brains in the human population. Even with the growth of teamwork and the attempted solution of future problems now coming to be known as systems analysis, man is our most recalcitrant material. He does not yield cherished beliefs with rapidity; he will not take pills at the decree of some distant, well-intentioned savior.

No one knows surely what was the purpose of Olmec art. We do know something of the seemingly endless political expansion and ethnic dilution that precipitated the fall of Rome. We know also that the pace of technological innovation in the modern world has multiplied throughout our lifetimes. The skills expended now upon space may in the end alter our philosophies and rewrite our dreams, even our very concepts of the nature of life—if there is life—beyond us in the void. Moreover the whole invisible pyramid is itself the incidental product of a primitive seed capsule, the human brain, whose motivations alter with time and circumstance.

In summary, we come round again to the human objective. In the first four million years of man's existence, or, even more pointedly, in the scant second's tick during which he has inhabited cities and devoted himself to an advanced technology, is it not premature to pronounce either upon his intentions or his destiny? Perhaps it is—as the first man-ape could not have foreseen the book-lined room in which I write. Yet something of that creature remains in me as he does in all men. I compose, or I make clever objects with what were originally a tree dweller's hands. Fragments of his fears, his angers, his desires, still stream like midnight shadows through the circuits of my brain. His unthinking jungle violence, inconceivably magnified, may determine our ending. Still, by contrast, the indefinable potentialities of a heavy-browed creature capable of pouring his scant wealth into the grave in a gesture of grief and self-abnegation may lead us at last to some triumph beyond the realm of technics. Who is to say?

Not long ago, seated upon a trembling ladder leading to a cliff-house ruin that has not heard the voice of man for centuries, I watched, in a puff of wind, a little swirl of silvery thistledown rise out of the canyon gorge beneath my feet. One or two seeds fell among stony crevices about me, but another, rising higher and higher upon the light air, ascended into the blinding sunshine beyond my vision. It is like man, I thought briefly, as I resumed my climb. It is like man, inside or out, off to new worlds where the chances, the stairways, are infinite. But like the seed, he has to grow. That impulse, too, we bring with us from the ancestral dark.

Another explosion of shimmering gossamer circled about my head. I held to the rickety ladder and followed the erratic, windborne flight of seeds until it mounted beyond the constricting canyon walls and vanished. Perhaps the eruption of our giant rockets into space had no more significance that this, I saw finally, as in a long geological perspective. It was only life engaged once more on an old journey. Here, perhaps, was our supreme objective, hidden by secretive nature even from ourselves.

Almost four centuries ago, Francis Bacon, in the years of the voyagers, had spoken of the new world of science as "something touching upon hope." In such hope do all launched seeds participate. And so did I, did unstable man upon his ladder or his star. It was no more than that. Within, without, the climb was many-dimensioned and over imponderable abysses. I placed my foot more carefully and edged one step farther up the face of the cliff.

The Last Magician

*The human heart is local and finite, it has
roots, and if the intellect radiates from it, according to its strength, to greater and greater
distances, the reports, if they are to be gathered
up at all, must be gathered at the center.*

GEORGE SANTAYANA

Every man in his youth—and who is to say when youth is ended?—
meets for the last time a magician, the man who made him what he is
finally to be. In the mass, man now confronts a similar magician in the
shape of his own collective brain, that unique and spreading force
which in its manipulations will precipitate the last miracle, or, like the
sorcerer's apprentice, wreak the last disaster. The possible nature of
the last disaster the world of today has made all too evident: man has
become a spreading blight which threatens to efface the green world
that created him.

It is of the last miracle, however, that I would write. To do so I have
to describe my closing encounter with the personal magician of my
youth, the man who set his final seal upon my character. To tell the
tale is symbolically to establish the nature of the human predicament:
how nature is to be reentered; how man, the relatively unthinking and
proud creator of the second world—the world of culture —may re-

vivify and restore the first world which cherished and brought him into being.

I was fifty years old when my youth ended, and it was, of all unlikely places, within that great unwieldy structure built to last forever and then hastily to be torn down—the Pennsylvania Station in New York. I had come in through a side doorway and was slowly descending a great staircase in a slanting shaft of afternoon sunlight. Distantly I became aware of a man loitering at the bottom of the steps, as though awaiting me there. As I descended he swung about and began climbing toward me.

At the instant I saw his upturned face my feet faltered and I almost fell. I was walking to meet a man ten years dead and buried, a man who had been my teacher and confidant. He had not only spread before me as a student the wild background of the forgotten past but had brought alive for me the spruce-forest primitives of today. With him I had absorbed their superstitions, handled their sacred objects, accepted their prophetic dreams. He had been a man of unusual mental powers and formidable personality. In all my experience no dead man but he could have so wrenched time as to walk through its cleft of darkness unharmed into the light of day.

The massive brows and forehead looked up at me as if to demand an accounting of that elapsed decade during which I had held his post and discharged his duties. Unwilling step by step I descended rigidly before the baleful eyes. We met, and as my dry mouth strove to utter his name, I was aware that he was passing me as a stranger, that his gaze was directed beyond me, and that he was hastening elsewhere. The blind eye turned sidewise was not, in truth, fixed upon me; I beheld the image but not the reality of a long dead man. Phantom or genetic twin, he passed on, and the crowds of New York closed inscrutably about him.

I groped for the marble railing and braced my continued descent. Around me travelers moved like shadows. I was a similar shadow, made so by the figure I had passed. But what was my affliction? That dead man and myself had been friends, not enemies. What terror save the terror of the living toward the dead could so powerfully have enveloped me?

On the slow train running homeward the answer came. I had been away for ten years from the forest. I had had no messages from its depths, such as that dead savant had hoarded even in his disordered office where box turtles wandered over the littered floor. I had been immersed in the postwar administrative life of a growing university. But all the time some accusing spirit, the familiar of the last wood-struck magician, had lingered in my brain. Finally exteriorized, he had stridden up the stair to confront me in the autumn light. Whether he had been imposed in some fashion upon a convenient facsimile or was a genuine illusion was of little importance compared to the message he had brought. I had starved and betrayed myself. It was this that had brought the terror. For the first time in years I left my office in mid-afternoon and sought the sleeping silence of a nearby cemetery. I was as pale and drained as the Indian pipe plants without chlorophyll that rise after rains on the forest floor. It was time for a change. I wrote a letter and studied timetables. I was returning to the land that bore me.

Collective man is now about to enter upon a similar though more difficult adventure. At the climactic moment of his journey into space he has met himself at the doorway of the stars. And the looming shadow before him has pointed backward into the entangled gloom of a forest from which it has been his purpose to escape. Man has crossed, in his history, two worlds. He must now enter another and forgotten one, but with the knowledge gained on the pathway to the moon. He must learn that, whatever his powers as a magician, he lies under the spell of a greater and a green enchantment which, try as he will, he can never avoid, however far he travels. The spell has been laid on him since the beginning of time—the spell of the natural world from which he sprang.

II

Long ago Plato told the story of the cave and the chained prisoners whose knowledge consisted only of what they could learn from flickering shadows on the wall before them. Then he revealed their astonishment upon being allowed to see the full source of the light. He concluded that the mind's eye may be bewildered in two ways, either from advancing suddenly into the light of higher things or descending once more from the light into the shadows. Perhaps more than Plato realized in the spinning of his myth, man has truly emerged from a cave of shadows, or from comparable leaf-shadowed dells. He has read his way into the future by firelight and by moonlight, for, in man's early history, night was the time for thinking, and for the observation of the stars. The stars traveled, men noted, and therefore they were given hunters' names. All things moved and circled. It was the way of the hunters' world and of the seasons.

In spite of much learned discourse upon the ways of our animal kin, and of how purely instinctive cries slowly gave way to variable and muddled meanings in the head of proto-man, I like to think that the crossing into man's second realm of received wisdom was truly a magical experience.

I once journeyed for several days along a solitary stretch of coast. By the end of that time, from the oddly fractured shells on the beach, little distorted faces began to peer up at me with meaning. I had held no converse with a living thing for many hours. As a result I was beginning, in the silence, to read again, to read like an illiterate. The reading had nothing to do with sound. The faces in the cracked shells were somehow assuming a human significance.

Once again, in the night, as I traversed a vast plain on foot, the clouds that coursed above me in the moonlight began to build into archaic, voiceless pictures. That they could do so in such a manner makes me sure that the reading of such pictures has long preceded what men of today call language. The reading of so endless an alphabet of forms is already beyond the threshold of the animal; man could somehow see a face in a shell or a pointing finger in a cloud. He had both magnified and contracted his person in a way verging on the uncanny. There existed in the growing cortex of man, in its endless ramifications and prolonged growth, a place where, paradoxically, time both flowed and lingered, where mental pictures multiplied and transposed themselves. One is tempted to believe, whether or not it is literally true, that the moment of first speech arrived in a star burst like a supernova. To be sure, the necessary auditory discrimination and memory tracts were a biological preliminary, but the "invention" of language—and I put this carefully, having respect for both the biological and cultural elements involved— may have come, at the last, with rapidity.

Certainly the fossil record of man is an increasingly strange one. Millions of years were apparently spent on the African and Asiatic grasslands, with little or no increase in brain size, even though simple tools were in use. Then quite suddenly in the million years or so of Ice Age time the brain cells multiply fantastically. One prominent linguist would place the emergence of true language at no more than forty thousand years ago. I myself would accord it a much longer history, but all scholars would have to recognize biological preparation for its emergence. What the fossil record, and perhaps even the studies of living primates, will never reveal is how much can be attributed to slow incremental speech growth associated directly with the expanding brain, and how much to the final cultural innovation spreading rapidly to other biologically prepared groups.

Language, wherever it first appeared, is the cradle of the human universe, a universe displaced from the natural in the common environmental sense of the word. In this second world of culture, forms arise in the brain and can be transmitted in speech as words are found for them. Objects and men are no longer completely within the world we call natural—they are subject to the transpositions which the brain can evoke or project. The past can be remembered and caused to haunt the present. Gods may murmur in the trees, or ideas of cosmic proportions can twine a web of sustaining mathematics around the cosmos.

In the attempt to understand his universe, man has to give away a part of himself which can never be regained —the certainty of the animal that what it senses is actually there in the shape the eye beholds. By contrast, man finds himself in Plato's cave of illusion. He has acquired an interest in the whole of the natural world at the expense of being ejected from it and returning, all too frequently, as an angry despoiler.

A distinction, however, should be made here. In his first symbol making, primitive man—and indeed even the last simple hunting cultures of today—projected a friendly image upon animals: animals talked among themselves and thought rationally like men; they had souls. Men might even have been fathered by totemic animals. Man was still existing in close interdependence with his first world, though already he had developed a philosophy, a kind of oracular "reading" of its nature. Nevertheless he was still inside that world; he had not turned it into an instrument or a mere source of materials.

Christian man in the West strove to escape this lingering illusion that the primitives had projected upon nature. Intent upon the destiny of his own soul, and increasingly urban, man drew back from too great intimacy with the natural, its fertility and its orgiastic attractions. If the new religion was to survive, Pan had to be driven from his hillside or rendered powerless by incorporating him into Christianity—to be baptized, in other words, and allowed to fade slowly from the memory of the folk. As always in such intellectual upheavals, something was gained and something lost.

What was gained intellectually was a monotheistic reign of law by a single deity so that man no longer saw distinct and powerful spirits in every tree or running brook. His animal confreres slunk like pariahs soulless from his presence. They no longer spoke, their influence upon man was broken; the way was unconsciously being prepared for the rise of modern science. That science, by reason of its detachment, would first of all view nature as might a curious stranger. Finally it would, while giving powers to man, turn upon him also the same gaze that had driven the animal forever into the forest. Man, too, would be subject to what he had evoked; he, too, in a new fashion, would be relegated soulless to the wood with all his lurking irrationalities exposed. He would know in a new and more relentless fashion his relationship to the rest of life. Yet as the growing crust of his exploitive technology thickened, the more man thought that he could withdraw from or recast nature, that by drastic retreat he could dispel his deepening sickness.

Like that of one unfortunate scientist I know—a remorseless experimenter—man's whole face had grown distorted. One eye, one bulging eye, the technological, scientific eye, was willing to count man as well as nature's creatures in terms of megadeaths. Its objectivity had become so great as to endanger its master, who was mining his own brains as ruthlessly as a seam of coal. At last Ortega y Gasset was to remark despairingly, "There is no human nature, there is only history." That history, drawn from man's own brain and subject to his power to transpose reality, now looms before us as future on all the confines of the world.

Linguists have a word for the power of language: displacement. It is the way by which man came to survive in nature. It is also the method by which he created and entered his second world, the realm that now encloses him. In addition, it is the primary instrument by which he developed the means to leave the planet earth. It is a very mysterious achievement whose source is none other than the ghostly symbols moving along the ramifying pathways of the human cortex, the gray enfolded matter of the brain. Displacement, in simple terms, is the ability to talk about what is absent, to make use of the imaginary in order to control reality. Man alone is able to manipulate time into past and future, transpose objects or abstract ideas in a similar fashion, and make a kind of reality which is not present, or which exists only as potential in the real world.

From this gift comes his social structure and traditions and even the tools with which he modifies his surroundings. They exist in the dark confines of the cranium before the instructed hand creates the reality. In addition, and as a corollary of displacement, language is characterized by the ability to receive constant increments and modifications. Words drop into or out of use, or change their meanings. The constant easy ingestion of the new, in spite of the stability of grammatical structure, is one of the prime characteristics of language. It is a structured instrument which at the same time reveals an amazing flexibility. This flexibility allows us a distant glimpse of the endlessly streaming shadows that make up the living brain.

III

There is another aspect of man's mental life which demands the utmost attention, even though it is manifest in different degrees in different times and places and among different individuals; this is the desire for transcendence—a peculiarly human trait. Philosophers and students of comparative religion have sometimes remarked that we need to seek for the origins of the human interest in the cosmos, "a cosmic sense" unique to man. However this sense may have evolved, it has made men of the greatest imaginative power conscious of human inadequacy and weakness. There may thus emerge the desire for "rebirth" expressed in many religions. Stimulated by his own uncompleted nature, man seeks a greater role, restructured beyond nature like so much in his aspiring mind. Thus we find the Zen Buddhist, in the words of the scholar Suzuki, intent upon creating "a realm of Emptiness or Void where no conceptualism prevails" and where "rootless trees grow." The Buddhist, in a true paradox, would empty the mind in order that the mind may adequately receive or experience the world. No other creature than man would question his way of thought or feel the need of sweeping the mind's cloudy mirror in order to unveil its insight.

Man's life, in other words, is felt to be unreal and sterile. Perhaps a creature of so much ingenuity and deep memory is almost bound to grow alienated from his world, his fellows, and the objects around him. He suffers from a nostalgia for which there is no remedy upon earth except as it is to be found in the enlightenment of the spirit— some ability to have a perceptive rather than an exploitive relationship with his fellow creatures.

After man had exercised his talents in the building of the first neolithic cities and empires, a period mostly marked by architectural and military triumphs, an intellectual transformation descended upon the known world, a time of questioning. This era is fundamental to an understanding of man, and has engaged the attention of such modern scholars as Karl Jaspers and Lewis Mumford. The period culminates in the first millennium before Christ. Here in the great centers of civilization, whether Chinese, Indian, Judaic, or Greek, man had begun to abandon inherited gods and purely tribal loyalties in favor of an inner world in which the pursuit of earthly power was ignored. The destiny of the human soul became of more significance than the looting of a province. Though these dreams are expressed in different ways by such divergent men as Christ, Buddha, Lao-tse, and Confucius, they share many things in common, not the least of which is respect for the dignity of the common man.

The period of the creators of transcendent values—the axial thinkers, as they are called—created the world of universal thought that is our most precious human heritage. One can see it emerging in the mind of Christ as chronicled by Saint John. Here the personalized tribal deity of earlier Judaic thought becomes transformed into a world deity. Christ, the Good Shepherd, says: "Other sheep I have, which are not of this fold: them also I must bring, and they shall hear my voice; and there shall be one fold and one shepherd.... My sheep hear my voice ... and they follow me."

These words spoken by the carpenter from Nazareth are those of a world changer. They passed boundaries, whispered in the ears of galley slaves: "One fold, one shepherd. Follow me." These are no longer the wrathful words of a jealous city ravager, a local potentate god. They mark instead, in the high cultures, the rise of a new human image, a rejection of purely material goals, a turning toward some inner light. As these ideas diffused, they were, of course, subject to the wear and time of superstition, but the human ethic of the individual prophets and thinkers has outlasted empires.

Such men speak to us across the ages. In their various approaches to life they encouraged the common man toward charity and humility. They did not come with weapons; instead they bespoke man's purpose to subdue his animal nature and in so doing to create a radiantly new and noble being. These were the dreams of the first millennium B.C. Tormented man, arising, falling, still pursues those dreams today.

Earlier I mentioned Plato's path into the light that blinds the man who has lived in darkness. Out of just such darkness arose the first humanizing influence. It was genuinely the time of the good shepherds. No one can clearly determine why these prophets had such profound effects within the time at their disposal. Nor can we solve the mystery of how they came into existence across the Euro-Asiatic land mass in diverse cultures at roughly the same time. As Jaspers observes, he who can solve this mystery will know something common to all mankind.

In this difficult era we are still living in the inspirational light of a tremendous historical event, one that opened up the human soul. But if the neophytes were blinded by the light, so, perhaps, the prophets were in turn confused by the human darkness they encountered. The scientific age replaced them. The common man, after brief days of enlightenment, turned once again to escape, propelled outward first by the world voyagers, and then by the atom breakers. We have called up vast powers which loom menacingly over us. They await our bidding, and we turn to outer space as though the solitary answer to the unspoken query must be flight, such flight as ancient man engaged in across ice ages and vanished game trails—the flight from nowhere.

The good shepherds meantime have all faded into the darkness of history. One of them, however, left a cryptic message: "My doctrine is not mine but his that sent me." Even in the time of unbelieving this carries a warning. For He that sent may still be couched in the body of man awaiting the end of the story.

IV

When I was a small boy I once lived near a brackish stream that wandered over the interminable salt flats south of our town. Between occasional floods the area became a giant sunflower forest, taller than the head of a man. Child gangs roved this wilderness, and guerrilla combats with sunflower spears sometimes took place when boys from the other side of the marsh ambushed the hidden trails. Now and then, when a raiding party sought a new path, one could see from high ground the sunflower heads shaking and closing over the passage of the life below. In some such manner nature's green barriers must have trembled and subsided in silence behind the footsteps of the first man-apes who stumbled out of the vine-strewn morass of centuries into the full sunlight of human consciousness.

The sunflower forest of personal and racial childhood is relived in every human generation. One reaches the high ground, and all is quiet in the shaken reeds. The nodding golden flowers spring up indifferently behind us, and the way backward is lost when finally we turn to look. There is something unutterably secretive involved in man's intrusion into his second world, into the mutable domain of thought. Perhaps he questions still his right to be there.

Some act unknown, some propitiation of unseen forces, is demanded of him. For this purpose he has raised pyramids and temples, but all in vain. A greater sacrifice is demanded, the act of a truly great magician, the man capable of transforming himself. For what, increasingly, is required of man is that he pursue the paradox of return. So desperate has been the human emergence from fen and thicket, so great has seemed the virtue of a single magical act carried beyond nature, that man hesitates, as long ago I had similarly shuddered to confront a phantom on a stair.

Written deep in the human subconscious is a simple terror of what has come with us from the forest and sometimes haunts our dreams. Man does not wish to retrace his steps down to the margin of the reeds and peer within, lest by some magic he be permanently recaptured. Instead, men prefer to hide in cities of their own devising. I know a New Yorker who, when she visits the country, complains that the crickets keep her awake. I knew another who had to be awakened screaming from a nightmare of whose nature he would never speak. As for me, a long-time student of the past, I, too, have had my visitants.

The dreams are true. By no slight effort have we made our way through the marshes. Something unseen has come along with each of us. The reeds sway shut, but not as definitively as we would wish. It is the price one pays for bringing almost the same body through two worlds. The animal's needs are very old; it must sometimes be coaxed into staying in its new discordant realm. As a consequence all religions have realized that the soul must not be allowed to linger yearning at the edge of the sunflower forest.

The curious sorcery of sound symbols and written hieroglyphs in man's new brain had to be made to lure him farther and farther from the swaying reeds. Temples would better contain his thought and fix his dreams upon the stars in the night sky. A creature who has once passed from visible nature into the ghostly insubstantial world evolved and projected from his own mind will never cease to pursue thereafter the worlds beyond this world. Nevertheless the paradox remains: man's crossing into the realm of space has forced him equally to turn and contemplate with renewed intensity the world of the sunflower forest —the ancient world of the body that he is doomed to inhabit, the body that completes his cosmic prison.

Not long ago I chanced to fly over a forested section of country which, in my youth, was still an unfrequented wilderness. Across it now suburbia was spreading. Below, like the fungus upon a fruit, I could see the radiating lines of transport gouged through the naked earth. From far up in the wandering air one could see the lines stretching over the horizon. They led to cities clothed in an unmoving haze of smog. From my remote, abstract position in the clouds I could gaze upon all below and watch the incipient illness as it spread with all its slimy tendrils through the watershed.

Farther out, I knew, on the astronauts' track, the earth would hang in silver light and the seas hold their ancient blue. Man would be invisible; the creeping white rootlets of his urban growth would be equally unseen. The blue, cloud-covered planet would appear still as when the first men stole warily along a trail in the forest. Upon one thing, however, the scientists of the space age have informed us. Earth is an inexpressibly unique possession. In the entire solar system it alone possesses water and oxygen sufficient to nourish higher life. It alone contains the seeds of mind. Mercury bakes in an inferno of heat beside the sun; something strange has twisted the destiny of Venus; Mars is a chill desert; Pluto is a cold wisp of reflected light over three billion miles away on the edge of the black void. Only on earth does life's green engine fuel the oxygen-devouring brain.

For centuries we have dreamed of intelligent beings throughout this solar system. We have been wrong; the earth we have taken for granted and treated so casually—the sunflower-shaded forest of man's infancy—is an incredibly precious planetary jewel. We are all of us—man, beast, and growing plant—aboard a space ship of limited dimensions whose journey began so long ago that we have abandoned one set of gods and are now in the process of substituting another in the shape of science.

The axial religions had sought to persuade man to transcend his own nature; they had pictured to him limitless perspectives of self-mastery. By contrast, science in our time has opened to man the prospect of limitless power over exterior nature. Its technicians sometimes seem, in fact, to have proffered us the power of the void as though flight were the most important value on earth.

"We have got to spend everything we have, if necessary, to get off this planet," one such representative of the aerospace industry remarked to me recently.

"Why?" I asked, not averse to flight, but a little bewildered by his seeming desperation.

"Because," he insisted, his face turning red as though from some deep inner personal struggle, "because"—then he flung at me what I suspect he thought my kind of science would take seriously—"because of the ice—the ice is coming back, that's why."

Finally, as though to make everything official, one of the space agency administrators was quoted in *Newsweek* shortly after the astronauts had returned from the moon: "Should man," this official said, "fall back from his destiny ... the confines of this planet will destroy him."

It was a strange way to consider our planet, I thought, closing the magazine and brooding over this sudden distaste for life at home. Why was there this hidden anger, this inner flight syndrome, these threats for those who remained on earth? Some powerful, not totally scientific impulse seemed tugging at the heart of man. Was it fear of his own mounting numbers, the creeping of the fungus threads? But where, then, did these men intend to flee? The solar system stretched bleak and cold and crater-strewn before my mind. The nearest, probably planetless star was four light years and many human generations away. I held up the magazine once more. Here and here alone, photographed so beautifully from space, was the blue jewel compounded of water and of living green. Yet upon the page the words repeated themselves: "This planet will destroy him."

No, I thought, this planet nourished man. It took four million years to find our way through the sunflower forest, and after that only a few millennia to reach the moon. It is not fair to say this planet will destroy us. Space flight is a brave venture, but upon the soaring rockets are projected all the fears and evasions of man. He had fled across two worlds, from the windy corridors of wild savannahs to the sunlit world of the mind, and still he flees. Earth will not destroy him. It is he who threatens to destroy the earth. In sober terms we are forced to reflect that by enormous expenditure and effort we have ventured a small way out into the planetary system of a minor star, but an even smaller way into the distances, no less real, that separate man from man.

Creatures who evolve as man has done sometimes bear the scar tissue of their evolutionary travels in their bodies. The human cortex, the center of high thought, has come to dominate, but not completely to suppress, the more ancient portions of the animal brain. Perhaps it was from this last wound that my engineer friend was unconsciously fleeing. We know that within our heads there still exists an irrational restive ghost that can whisper disastrous messages into the ear of reason.

During the axial period, as we have noted, several great religions arose in Asia. For the first time in human history man's philosophical thinking seems to have concerned itself with universal values, with man's relation to man across the barriers of empire or tribal society. A new ethic, not even now perfected, struggled to emerge from the human mind. To these religions of self-sacrifice and disdain of worldly power men were drawn in enormous numbers. Though undergoing confused erosion in our time, they still constitute the primary allegiance of many millions of the world's population.

Today man's mounting numbers and his technological power to pollute his environment reveal a single demanding necessity: the necessity for him consciously to reenter and preserve, for his own safety, the old first world from which he originally emerged. His second world, drawn from his own brain, has brought him far, but it cannot take him out of nature, nor can he live by escaping into his second world alone. He must now incorporate from the wisdom of the axial thinkers an ethic not alone directed toward his fellows, but extended to the living world around him. He must make, by way of his cultural world, an actual conscious reentry into the sunflower forest he had thought merely to exploit or abandon. He must do this in order to survive. If he succeeds he will, perhaps, have created a third world which combines elements of the original two and which should bring closer the responsibilities and nobleness of character envisioned by the axial thinkers who may be acclaimed as the creators, if not of man, then of his soul. They expressed, in a prescientific era, man's hunger to transcend his own image, a hunger not entirely submerged even beneath the formidable weaponry and technological triumphs of the present.

The story of the great saviors, whether Chinese, Indian, Greek, or Judaic, is the story of man in the process of enlightening himself, not simply by tools, but through the slow inward growth of the mind that made and may yet master them through knowledge of itself. "The poet, like the lightning rod," Emerson once stated, "must reach from a point nearer the sky than all surrounding objects down to the earth, and into the dark wet soil, or neither is of use." Today that effort is demanded not only of the poet. In the age of space it is demanded of all of us. Without it there can be no survival of mankind, for man himself must be his last magician. He must seek his own way home.

The task is admittedly gigantic, but even Halley's flaming star has rounded on its track, a pinpoint of light in the uttermost void. Man, like the comet, is both bound and free. Throughout the human generations the star has always turned homeward. Nor do man's inner journeys differ from those of that far-flung elliptic. Now, as in earlier necromantic centuries, the meteors that afflicted ignorant travelers rush overhead. In the ancient years, when humankind wandered through briars and along windy precipices, it was thought well, when encountering comets or firedrakes, "to pronounce the name of God with a clear voice."

This act was performed once more by many millions when the wounded Apollo 13 swerved homeward, her desperate crew intent, if nothing else availed, upon leaving their ashes on the winds of earth. A love for earth, almost forgotten in man's roving mind, had momentarily reasserted its mastery, a love for the green meadows we have so long taken for granted and desecrated to our cost. Man was born and took shape among earth's leafy shadows. The most poignant thing the astronauts had revealed in their extremity was the nostalgic call still faintly ringing on the winds from the sunflower forest.

Loren, age six and a half, and his mom, Daisy.
Courtesy of University of Pennsylvania Archives

South Party group picture, *left to right:* Bert Schultz, Mylan Stout, Emery Blue, Robert Long, Loren Eiseley, Eugene Vanderpool, and Frank Crabill. *Courtesy of University of Pennsylvania Archives*

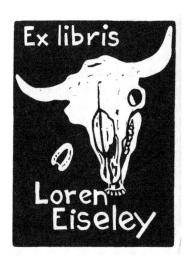

Bookplate created by Loren for his book collection. *Courtesy of University of Pennsylvania Archives*

Loren excavating a storage pit from a historic Kansas Indian village, July 1937. *Courtesy of University of Pennsylvania Archives*

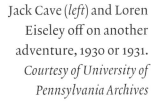

Jack Cave (*left*) and Loren Eiseley off on another adventure, 1930 or 1931. *Courtesy of University of Pennsylvania Archives*

Loren's mom, Daisy, at an advanced age.
Courtesy of University of Pennsylvania Archives

Dorothy Thomas, Loren Eiseley, and Mabel Langdon, Loren's fiancée, in Holy Ghost Canyon, New Mexico (southeast of Santa Fe). *Courtesy of University of Pennsylvania Archives*

Loren's high school graduation picture. *Courtesy of University of Pennsylvania Archives*

Mabel Langdon and friend Elizabeth Cave Fer-
rier, 1932 in Nebraska City, Nebraska. *Courtesy of
University of Pennsylvania Archives*

Portrait of Mabel Langdon. *Courtesy of University of Pennsylvania Archives*

Loren's dad, Clyde
Eiseley, and his second
wife, Effie "Eva"
Cearns. *Courtesy of Uni-*
versity of Pennsylvania
Archives

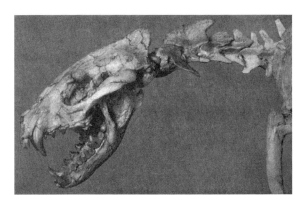

Sunkahetanka Geringensis. Found in 1931 by Blue,
Crabill, Eiseley, and Schultz at Redington Gap,
west of Bridgeport, Nebraska. *Courtesy of The*
Univerity of Nebraska State Museum

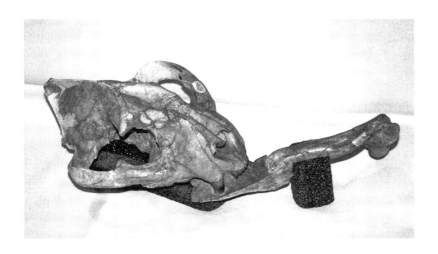

Found in 1932 by Loren Eiseley and Frank Crabill, "The Innocent Assassins" fossil, estimated to be twenty-five million years old, has the tibia of one *Nimravus brachyops* impaled by the large canines of another. *Courtesy of Bing Chen (photo taken at the University of Nebraska Medical Center)*

Loren in his office at the University of Pennsylvania. *Courtesy of University of Pennsylvania Archives*

Loren at the Wildcat Hills escarpment, Nebraska. *Courtesy of University of Pennsylvania Archives*

Portrait of Loren. *Courtesy of University of Pennsylvania Archives*

LOREN EISELEY'S
NEBRASKA

including other famous Nebraska fossils

Clash of the Mammoths
Mammuthus columbi
Trailside Museum of Natural History
at Ft. Robinson State Park

Western Nebraska – "The Judgment of the Birds," "The Slit"

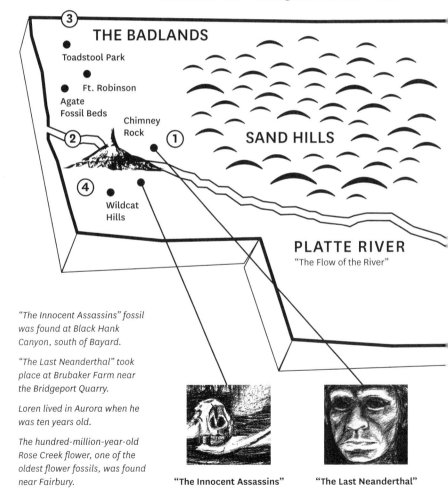

③
THE BADLANDS
Toadstool Park

● Ft. Robinson
Agate
Fossil Beds
Chimney
② Rock ①

SAND HILLS

④
Wildcat
Hills

PLATTE RIVER
"The Flow of the River"

*"The Innocent Assassins" fossil
was found at Black Hank
Canyon, south of Bayard.*

*"The Last Neanderthal" took
place at Brubaker Farm near
the Bridgeport Quarry.*

*Loren lived in Aurora when he
was ten years old.*

*The hundred-million-year-old
Rose Creek flower, one of the
oldest flower fossils, was found
near Fairbury.*

"The Innocent Assassins"   **"The Last Neanderthal"**

Among Eiseley and South Party Discoveries

① **Morrill County – Redington Gap, Black Hank Canyon, and Bridgeport Quarry**
found: *Mammuthus columbi* (mammoth), *Menoceras falkenbachi* (crescent horned rhino), *Nimravus brachyops* (saber-toothed nimravid), *Sespia marianae* (oreodont), *Sunkahetanka geringensis* (Gering's large-toothed dog)

② **Scotts Bluff County – Bison Quarry near Signal Butte**
found: *Bison occidentalis* (bison), *Canis* sp. (near *C. latrans*, coyote), *Mesohippus bairdi* (small horse), Paleoindian artifacts (including dart points and tools)

③ **Sioux County – Areas north of Harrison and northwest of Crawford**
found: *Bison* sp. (bison), *Brontops* (brontothere), camel, fossilized eggs, *Hyaenodon horridus* (creodont), *Mesohippus* (small horse), oreodont, *Palaeocastor* (burrowing beaver), saber-toothed carnivore, *Subhyracodon tridactylum* (hornless rhino), turtle

④ **Banner County – Faden Quarry, located east of Harrisburg**
found: beardog (amphicyonid), camel, *Eubelodon morrilli* (perfect-tusk gomphothere), *Peraceras crassus* (hornless rhino), saber-toothed carnivore

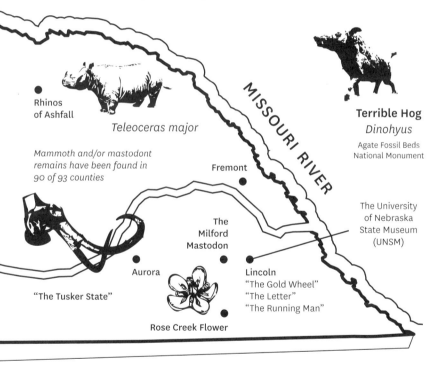

Rhinos
of Ashfall

Teleoceras major

Mammoth and/or mastodont
remains have been found in
90 of 93 counties

Fremont

The
Milford
Mastodon

Aurora

"The Tusker State"

Rose Creek Flower

Terrible Hog
Dinohyus

Agate Fossil Beds
National Monument

The University
of Nebraska
State Museum
(UNSM)

Lincoln
"The Gold Wheel"
"The Letter"
"The Running Man"

Thunder Beast
Brontops Sioux County

*Eiseley was with the UNSM South Party
in 1931, 1932, and 1933.*

*1910, Loren sees Halley's Comet while
in Fremont, where he lived until the
age of three.*

*March 14, 1912, three convicts
escape from the Nebraska State
Penitentiary in Lincoln.*

Bibliography

All the Strange Hours: The Excavation of a Life. New York: Charles Scribner's Sons, 1975. Prose.

The Brown Wasps (private edition). Mount Horeb, Wis.: The Perishable Press Ltd., 1969. Prose.

Darwin's Century: Evolution and the Men Who Discovered It. New York: Doubleday and Co., 1958. Prose.

Francis Bacon and the Modern Dilemma. Lincoln: University of Nebraska Press, 1962. Prose.

The Firmament of Time. New York: Atheneum Publishers, 1960. Prose.

The Innocent Assassins. New York: Charles Scribner's Sons, 1973. Poetry.

The Immense Journey. New York: Random House, 1957. Prose.

The Invisible Pyramid. New York: Charles Scribner's Sons, 1970. Prose.

The Mind as Nature. New York, Evanston, London: Harper & Row, 1962. Prose.

The Man Who Saw Through Time (revised and enlarged edition of *Francis Bacon and the Modern Dilemma*). New York: Charles Scribner's Sons, 1973. Prose.

Man, Time, and Prophecy (private Christmas edition). New York: Harcourt, Brace & World, 1966. Prose.

Notes of an Alchemist. New York: Charles Scribner's Sons, 1972. Prose.

The Night Country. New York: Charles Scribner's Sons, 1971. Prose.

The Unexpected Universe. New York: Harcourt, Brace & World, 1969. Prose.

Posthumous Books by Eiseley

Another Kind of Autumn. New York: Charles Scribner's Sons, 1977. Poetry.

All the Night Wings. New York: Times Books, 1980. Poetry.

Darwin and the Mysterious Mr. X: New Light on the Evolutionists. New York: E. P. Dutton, 1979. Prose.

The Lost Notebooks of Loren Eiseley. Lincoln: University of Nebraska Press, 2002. Poetry and prose.

The Star Thrower. New York: Times Books, 1978. Poetry and prose.

Biography on Eiseley

Christianson, Gale E. *Fox at the Wood's Edge*. Lincoln and London: University of Nebraska Press, 1990. Prose.

Acknowledgments

The publication of *The Loren Eiseley Reader* could not have been undertaken without the generous support of many individuals and organizations. First and foremost are the directors of The Loren Eiseley Society, coming from a rich diversity of backgrounds from the humanities to the sciences, who have given their unwavering support in spite of the many hurdles and challenges of this project. Among them, Cris Trautner and Aaron Vacin are responsible for the *Reader's* layout; choosing our artist, Aaron Franco; endless copyediting; and the selection of our printer. Then there is Deborah Derrick, who provided countless hours of her time in all phases of the *Reader's* creation, from essay selection to written communications, grant application preparation, and serving as a primary sounding board for all of us, especially the society's president, Bing Chen. Jim Cook and Kira Gale assisted with essay selection.

The Loren Eiseley Society wishes to thank Mr. Ray Bradbury for his gracious and enthusiastic support in writing the foreword, and to thank him for being the first to recognize the great talent that Loren Eiseley possessed and encouraging him to become an author.

The Loren Eiseley Society extends its sincere gratitude to Mark Frazier Lloyd, director of the University Archives and Records Center of the University of Pennsylvania, who serves as the custodian of the Loren Eiseley Estate, for granting permission to reprint the essays contained in *The Loren Eiseley Reader*.

We wish to acknowledge the Peter Kiewit Foundation's financial support via a challenge grant and its director, Lyn Zygenbein, for her guidance and mentoring on this project. We recognize the generous support by Mr. Hod Kosman, president of the Platte Valley State Bank of Scottsbluff, Nebraska, as the first private contributor to this effort.

We wish to thank Mr. Ray Boice for connecting western Nebraska and his vision of the Fossil Freeway to The Loren Eiseley Society. Also, we wish to thank the staff of the Heritage Room of the Lincoln City Libraries, especially Stephen Cloyd, for their assistance in the selection of photographs for this book.

Most of all, we wish to thank Loren Corey Eiseley for his gift of lyrical prose with its inspirational vision, a clairvoyance needed, and a message to be heeded if humankind intends to survive from this instant in geological time to the next, to perform again on the giant stage of life on Earth.

The Loren Eiseley Society Board of Directors:

Bing Chen (President)
Deborah Derrick (Secretary)
Morrie Tuttle (Treasurer)

James Cook, Kira Gale, Christine Lesiak, Thomas Lynch, Susan Maher, Cris Trautner, and Aaron Vacin

The Loren Eiseley Society Senior Advisory Board:

Darrel Berg, Gale Christianson, Scott Slovic, Mary Liz Jameson, and Barbara W. Sommer

The Loren Eiseley Society | www.eiseley.org